The Richer Way

Julian Richer established Richer Sounds in 1978. His business now turns over in excess of £200 million a year, and Richer Sounds has won the prestigious *Which?* Best Retailer award (2010, 2011 and 2015). In 2011 Richer Sounds was granted a Royal Warrant by HRH The Prince of Wales for the supply of consumer electronic products to the Royal Household. The first shop to be opened, near London Bridge, has for over 20 years been listed in Guinness World Records as achieving the highest sales per square foot of any retail outlet in the world. Fifteen per cent of the company's profits are donated to charitable causes (over 400 of them in 2017). In addition to his commercial activities, Julian Richer is the founder and a trustee of Acts 435, set up to help those in need, and in 2013 he established ASB Help, which works with victims of anti-social behaviour. He lives in Yorkshire.

Praise for *The Richer Way*

'Read this book and transform your business.'

Archie Norman

'Like all good management books, it is readable, controversial, and full of golden nuggets of good advice.'

Tim Daniels

'I first came across Richer Sounds many years ago when I read Julian Richer's book *The Richer Way*. His book was so full of common sense that I filled several pages of an A4 pad with his ideas. The i⋯ work.'

'Julian Richer has perfec⋯

T0099398

Also by Julian Richer

The Ethical Capitalist: How to Make Business
Work Better for Society

The Richer Way

How to Get the Best Out of People

JULIAN RICHER

1 3 5 7 9 10 8 6 4 2

Random House Business
20 Vauxhall Bridge Road
London SW1V 2SA

Random House Business is part of the Penguin Random
House group of companies whose addresses can be found at
global.penguinrandomhouse.com.

Penguin
Random House
UK

First published by Richer Publishing in 1995
This edition first published by Random House Business in 2020

www.penguin.co.uk

A CIP catalogue record for this book is available from the British
Library.

ISBN 9781847942234

Printed and bound in Great Britain by Clays Ltd, Elcograf S.p.A.

Penguin Random House is committed to a sustainable future for our
business, our readers and our planet. This book is made from Forest
Stewardship Council® certified paper.

MIX
Paper from
responsible sources
FSC® C018179

Dear Reader,

I am flattered that you have bought this book, but it is of great concern to me that you are pleased with your purchase.

If, for any reason, you feel after reading it that it did not provide value for money, please return it to me for a full, no quibble refund.

Julian Richer
Freepost SE5508
London SE1 4BR

I would like to dedicate this book to my dear parents, my late housemaster at Clifton, Ernest Polack, my late partner Vic Odden and my friend Archie Norman, all of whom have had a huge influence on me.

And especially to my wonderful wife, Rosie, who has supported me through thick and thin for many happy years.

Contents

Acknowledgements

I gave a talk to the senior management of EMAP in November 1993 and, afterwards, Colin Morrison, then chairman of EMAP Business Communications, suggested I write a book about my ideas.

Although I had vaguely considered it, he must take the credit for the inspiration to get the ball rolling. His supportive follow-up gave me the confidence to carry it through.

As well as this, he introduced me to Paul Keenan, who was at that stage the managing director of EMAP fashion, and who was to become my mentor, editor and more for the whole project. From introducing me to publishers, all the way through to jacket design at the end, he really was a great support.

Paul also introduced me to journalist Kate Miller, who helped me organise my ideas and establish a framework for the book, and whose experience and skill with the English language assisted me in getting my message over.

A thank you also to Anna, David and James, who waded through the various proofs in their own time, and for the valuable advice they gave me.

Now 24 years on, at the time of writing in 2017, comes a major revamp for this sixth edition, with the kind input of Nigel Wilcockson and his team at Penguin Random House.

I'd like to thank Jonny Clayton, our ops director, for checking that I got my facts right, and my long-suffering PA Teresa, who has painstakingly updated every page to ensure that this book is as up to date as it can be.

Also, thank you to Rosie Wills for proofing the final copy.

Finally, thanks to Rosie, my wife, without whose support nothing would be possible.

Introduction

When I bought and sold my first turntable at the age of fourteen I had no idea that one day I would be the biggest retailer of hi-fi equipment in Britain, that my shops would be declared the busiest in the world by *The Guinness Book of Records*[*] for twenty-plus years running and that the chief executives of some of the biggest organisations in the country would be asking my advice.

Had I known that then I would probably have been even more obnoxious.

Like many entrepreneurs I was a poor performer at school – though I managed to avoid actually getting expelled. I was provided with a good upbringing by my parents, but blessed with certainly no more than the average number of brain cells, and I'm definitely not a workaholic.

It is precisely because of this that I think this book was worth writing – to give encouragement

[*] Highest sales per square foot.

and support to people who maybe lack confidence and aren't academically brilliant, but still have the skills to provide a profitable service, to create jobs we badly need and to generate taxes to support the society we live in.

I also hope that established businesspeople and managers in other structures will find it thought-provoking and ultimately beneficial, because managing people is the key to success in any organisation.

This is not a long book because essentially the message is a simple one. I hope you enjoy what follows, but if you have any queries or comments, please do not hesitate to get in touch.

1

Getting out of the Stone Age

Now we are in the twenty-first century and most employers are still in the Stone Age. No matter how many books they have read and how much technology they have bought, the managers of many organisations in this country are primitive in their understanding of the most important part of their business – the people. They think they can run their company and make money, while they ignore the needs and wishes of their customers and staff. They're wrong.

Anyone in business, even starting out, can see that competition is getting fiercer and pressure on costs is growing. A successful business has to stand out above the competition and get the maximum from its resources. These days that applies just as much in the public sector – hospitals and schools, for instance, need to get the utmost out of limited resources.

That's obvious, but how do you do it?

I've put a great deal of effort into my own business to find the answer to that question, and in the process I have learnt a lot that can also benefit other organisations. As a consultant I have already been able to bring my ideas to a number of other companies, which have taken up many key suggestions and put them into practice. Now, through this book, I want to introduce my way of business – the Richer Way – to a wider audience.

I am not just talking about selling hi-fis. Naturally, I approach things from a retail point of view, but this book is not only for retailers. No organisation, manager or employer can afford to ignore certain fundamental questions: how do you get the best out of your workforce? How can you develop the right culture within your organisation? How can your organisation be constantly improving?

These are essential issues for everyone in commerce, industry and services to address. I don't only mean essential for the sake of the business profits; I would go so far as to say they are essential for the health of society too. When I say we need to get out of the Stone Age, it's because I feel we would have a more civilised society if we learnt to think more intelligently about people and discovered how to treat our employees and our customers better.

Some chapters here, such as Chapter 8, will perhaps be of greater interest to retailers like me, as I go into detail about how to treat customers from the moment they walk through the door. However, these days everyone from building societies to dentists recognises they have customers too, and I hope there are snippets in these practical chapters that people in other types of organisation can use.

A lot has been written about how to succeed in business – mostly by people who have never run a company in their lives. You can search for clues in the autobiographies of the rich and famous, but somehow they never tell you the real secrets in between relating how they got their knighthoods.

While a great deal of business success does come down to the drive, skill and luck of the individual, there is much more that organisations can do – regardless of their size and sector – but to do it they'll need to turn some cherished business assumptions on their heads.

I have learnt from the ups and downs of my own business and, as a consultant advising on customer care, I've also had an insight into a wide range of other businesses. The lesson everywhere is the same: focus on people.

Once you start looking at the people, priorities change and you find yourself out of step with the rest of the business world.

I've been accused of being quirky for some of the things Richer Sounds does, but to see these as gimmicks is to miss the point. There are very good reasons why holiday homes for staff are more important than leather chairs in the boardroom and why our employees work in tiny, crowded shops, but get the opportunity to ride around in a Bentley.

Most businesses make the mistake of measuring performance in terms of figures when they ought to be measuring it in terms of people. The primary measure of a business's success should be customer and staff satisfaction, not profits. Profits are simply an indicator that you are getting customer service right.

Anyone can play around with prices to push up sales and turnover. You can mess around with margins and hammer costs to make profits look good, but these are short-term tricks. Unless the customer is happy, the business will not last.

British businesses – with some honourable exceptions – have taken a long time to come to the realisation that they have to put the customer first. Now they need to act fast if they want to keep those customers. The public is becoming better informed and fussier. Firms that fall down on customer satisfaction will get left behind.

However, customer service is very low down on the list of priorities in most industries. You rarely see a customer services director on a company board. Customer service is usually left to a manager who reports to the marketing director. The signal those companies are sending out is that customer services is an afterthought.

A lot of British organisations resist the idea of customer service. They think of it as an American import and argue that customers won't be fooled by an insincere smile and a 'Have a nice day'.

It is true that customers won't be impressed if there is no real commitment to service underneath, but customer satisfaction is not just about smiles and name badges: it should drive every aspect of the business. If your prices are too high, that is not good service. If your product is unreliable, that is not good service.

Customer service means organising the business for the benefit of the customer, not for the benefit of the managers, factory production schedules or shareholders. It means treating customers as people who have needs that you must meet.

It's a simple idea, but not one that many companies succeed in putting into practice. In this book I want to describe what actions you can take to put the customer at the heart of your business.

Customers are not the only people on whom the success of your business depends. What about all the other people you deal with and rely on, from suppliers to bank managers? It is amazing how many managers treat them all as a nuisance, to be either fobbed off or grovelled to, when seeing them as people, with their own legitimate requirements, can make a big difference to the success of the business.

However, the most important and most neglected people in any business are the employees. And the most important and most neglected of these are the ones who actually deal with customers.

I have worked as a consultant for more than forty companies, from a sewage equipment manufacturer to the biggest national retailers. Time and again I've found that if a business has problems with customer service, it comes back to how that company treats its staff.

The product is irrelevant: the key to success is always how you treat people, so that they are motivated, productive and, in turn, treat your customers well.

Many managers know this and are looking for ways to better employees, but the level of thinking is still pretty primitive. They think offering a pension scheme and a company car makes them a caring employer, but they don't understand how to motivate their staff and how to ensure they do a good job, every time.

I believe work should be fun. I also think we should do less of it.

Managers and junior staff ought to enjoy coming into work and they should do a productive day's work when they are there. They should not have to stay until late at night or come in at weekends just to do their jobs. That's now the norm in many organisations, but at Richer Sounds people have to answer to me if they are caught working six days a week without a very good reason – and we're just as profitable.

It's not how long you work but how well you work that counts. If your people are not productive, that is because you are failing to motivate and control them.

Lessons from the most successful companies have shown how important control is. Whatever business you are in, the aim should be to find the best procedures and make sure everyone uses them, but control becomes sterile and restrictive unless people have motivation too.

Too many organisations have a fundamental lack of understanding of what motivates people. Motivation comes down to some basic things, like a pay structure that rewards performance or a suggestions scheme that rewards initiative.

The trick is to link the rewards to the aims of the business.

Companies do not maximise their potential – and could ultimately fail – because they don't reward what they really want their staff to do.

They claim to want good customer service, but that is not what they reward. They hire and promote on the basis of qualifications, gender or what school people went to. Pay rises reward length of service, and commissions and bonuses reward sales volume, turnover or market share.

Take the banking industry, which traditionally had a booming business. They rewarded their salespeople with massive commissions and so their people sold products, especially loans, which weren't right for their customers. In the mid 2000s it became clear that an unknown number of customers wouldn't be able to repay their debts, which subsequently led to the crash of the banking system and resulted in a worldwide recession.

If those salespeople had been rewarded, not just for sales, but also for customer satisfaction and suitability of the product, none of that would have happened.

Failing to understand people means that many employers send the wrong message to their staff, and they then wonder why they do not get the outcome they want. For instance, many companies are now keen to have more women in senior management positions. They are genuinely committed to this, but I find they have not questioned the unspoken messages they still send to their female staff. Why do they call management meetings at seven in the morning or seven at night when many women have childcare commitments? Why does the social club only organise five-a-side football matches and why do board members refer to all managers as 'him' and to junior staff as 'her'?

These might appear to be trivial details, but they undermine a company's efforts to change. However much the directors are saying to women, 'We want you at the top of this organisation', the unspoken message is: 'Your place is at the bottom'.

This book will show you how to go about sending the right messages to people and how to get the right results. There is no perfect formula for success. At Richer Sounds we do not claim to have all the answers. We've made mistakes and we still make them, but we try to learn from those mistakes, to refine our approach and to improve all the time.

The zest for continuous improvement is essential to any type of organisation. One of the main ways I seek to get that in my company is through our suggestion scheme – an overlooked tool in most organisations. At Richer Sounds the suggestion scheme is not just something employees get told about on their first day and never hear of again. It is not just a box in the corner of the office that is never used, or a way of patronising employees by inviting suggestions from them that the company never intends to implement. It is the engine of self-improvement in our company. Ideas come from the people and they power the company forward.

Organisations talk a lot about improvement, but are they really committed to it? Any company that says it wants to get better all the time, but which does not have a vibrant, successful suggestion scheme is wasting its time.

Businesses need to change. In the UK we don't think work ought to be fun. We believe there are the managers and the managed, and never the twain shall meet. And we think success is vulgar.

Well, guess what – a lot of businesses are staffed with people who are bored out of their minds and have no respect for their bosses, while the company struggles to survive.

It doesn't have to be like that and this book aims to show you how and why.

I don't claim that it tells you all you need to know to make your organisation perfect. There will be many other factors involved in success. Businesses tend to rise and fall, usually having their own life cycle, and I expect mine will be no exception. Irrespective of that, these principles apply to everyone and, unlike other management theories, they won't go out of date.

Focusing on people requires listening to what they are telling you, paying attention to individuals and finding out what messages you are sending them.

It needs action. I can't guarantee it will be easy, but I can tell you it will work.

I have drawn on my own experience and, while the principles are universal, different industries will put them into practice in different ways. Some of the things we do at Richer Sounds may be relevant to your organisation, others won't. You don't have to take your managers potholing or provide a flat in Paris for your staff (well, maybe not on day one), but this book should give you a lot of ideas on what to do to get your own organisation into the twenty-first century.

2

Managing and motivating

When I visited companies as a consultant I did something unusual – I talked to the staff. I always made a point of talking to a range of employees, in depth and without their managers present. I asked them how they felt about their jobs, what problems they saw and how they thought things could be improved.

If you ask the right questions, and if people know they can talk freely and confidentially, a flood of information pours out. From this flood I picked out the valuable nuggets, which told me how that organisation could improve its business.

Some of what I heard was personal gripes and grumbles, but much of it was people's unhappiness and frustration with the job, which any business needs to address if it wants good morale in the workforce. Staff also told me about procedures not being followed and standards not being met; and they had a lot to say on how those mistakes could be put right. I assessed this and drew out what was commercially viable.

Many of the companies I have worked for are among Britain's most successful and progressive, but I have not yet found a company where there is no room for improvement in morale and productivity. And the key to making that improvement is always to treat staff better.

In the worst cases, I have talked to workforces that were seriously unhappy and found standards that were dangerously low.

I am sure my anecdotal evidence is pretty representative of companies up and down the country. An interesting international study by a group of scientists, Associates for Research into the Science of Employment, found precious little enjoyment in British offices.

Their research discovered that white-collar workers in the UK felt significantly more stressed at work than their counterparts in other European countries. More than a third of the employees in the study felt they were not appreciated at work and only just over half had confidence in the ability of their managers.

As an employer, you might take the view that it is not your problem whether people are happy at work or not. You pay them, what more do they want? There are always plenty of others out there who can fill that post.

This is a very short-sighted attitude. For a start, pay is only one of the factors that motivate people. There are a host of other ways you can create better job satisfaction among your employees – and you owe it to your business to do that. The 'hire and fire' attitude has no place in an organisation that is serious about service to its customers.

Respect for the individual has always been a guiding principle for me as an employer. I think 'do as you would be done by' should apply as much at work as in any other area of life. This is not some touchy-feely waffle, but sound business sense. Trying to be a good employer does help me sleep better at night – but the profits of my business also speak for themselves.

My experience demonstrates that treating your staff better will make your business perform better. It is no good saying you cannot afford to look after your staff: you can't afford not to.

I know I'm going against the trend here. Instead of learning to treat employees as people, more and more companies are seeing them as a cost, and costs have to be cut.

Too many businesses now think that making a profit is about reducing overheads. This is ridiculously short-term thinking. To take this to the extreme – if you decide that your supermarket will have only one of its thirty checkouts operating on a Saturday, you will be able to show a wonderful profit that day, but you will not find many customers coming back after they have queued at the till for six hours!

You can cut costs again and again, but if customer service suffers then your business will suffer.

Too many companies completely misunderstand the importance of their employees. They think they can save money by 'empowering' staff, which is usually jargon for making fewer people do the same amount of work.

They start stripping out layers of management, failing to see that good management is essential for a successful business. When management structures are flattened, some of the best people leave, taking years of training and experience with them, while those who stay get frustrated and apathetic as they see their career paths fade away.

Have employers thought about what it means for their workforce to see no future, no opportunities to move upwards and better their position? Demoralisation and stagnation will set in.

Another favourite cost-cutting exercise is to replace full-time staff with part-timers on zero-hour contracts.

Part-time working can be useful and convenient for both the employer and the employee, but when firms turn full-time jobs into part-time ones simply to make savings at their staff's expense, they are making a mistake. If they opt for less experienced, lower paid staff, customer service will decline.

These current trends are dangerous. Before you know it, you have 'empowered' front-line staff who do not know what they are supposed to be doing and make it up as they go along, with too few managers to exert any control. You end up with confusion and stress, customer service suffers and, in the long term, profitability will fall.

Employers should stop and think about some of the other costs they could cut. How much do absenteeism and sickness cost? What about theft – or 'shrinkage', as we call it in the retail trade? The British Retail Consortium, in its annual survey of retail crime, found that in 2006–7 workers stole almost as much as shoplifters. Shops lost 1–2 per cent of their turnover in staff theft. Isn't that a cost worth cutting?

Retail is not the only industry to suffer from theft and fraud. If other organisations want to do something about these losses, they need to look at the way they treat their staff, as well as tightening up their controls. Employees steal if they have no respect for the company, or if they feel resentful and undervalued.

At Richer Sounds we have shrinkage less than a tenth of the average level for the retail industry. We also have lower absenteeism through sickness. Our absenteeism rate is 1–2 per cent, compared to a UK average of 4–5 per cent.

We have a very low labour turnover: once people have settled into a job with us, they stay, which means we also save on recruitment and training costs.

So the payback on treating people well is phenomenal when you start to measure it. Accountants are very good at calculating the return on capital invested in buildings, machinery and so on, but organisations do not bother to measure the payback on their investment in people.

Once you do consider it, you can see the value of your investment. A lot of businesses will look at my company and say it's all very well for Richer Sounds to provide holiday homes and a hardship fund for its staff, but we can't afford that sort of thing. My answer is that just reducing shrinkage by 1 per cent of our turnover saves nearly two million pounds every year. That pays for quite a few holiday homes.

However, it's no good introducing piecemeal incentives to solve, say, a labour turnover problem. If you do not value your staff and are not committed to them, they won't be bought off with a few goodies.

Respect for people has to be at the heart of your organisation. Only then will you have a well-motivated and productive workforce. Only then will that flow into good customer service and only then will your business prosper.

One of the most significant things we ever did at Richer Sounds was to change the way we refer to our employees. Within the company, we call everyone 'colleagues' rather than 'staff' or 'employees'. We chose this term in preference to the American 'associates' or 'partners' and we use it as much as possible. It is friendly but businesslike and puts everyone on equal terms.

I once recommended this to a huge company I was advising as a way of tackling the gulf that existed there between managers and junior staff. The chief executive was strongly in favour of the idea, but others were not so sure at first and when he referred to 'colleagues' at meetings everyone was tittering. When I went back to this company a year later, the concept of 'colleagues' had been adopted by everybody, and it is still in use there twenty-five years later! In the end, a simple difference in terminology probably created more cultural change in that company than anything else I recommended.

If you as a manager think of your team as colleagues, your attitude towards them will gradually change. Using this term generates respect throughout the organisation.

I hear lots of excuses from employers as to why it is not worth their while investing anything in their staff. People are unpredictable and ungrateful, they say. You send them on an expensive training course and then two months later they leave to join a competitor. You introduce some good perks, but after a while staff just take them for granted.

Some firms say they cannot attract good staff, the work is dull and repetitive and no one wants to do it. Others think they are stuck with poor workers they can't get rid of. 'If only we could set up a new factory and recruit from scratch,' they say, 'we would have the perfect workforce.'

All these excuses are indications of poor management rather than an unreliable workforce. I find employers are very quick to blame their staff for every problem.

In reality, you get very different output from people depending on how you manage and motivate them. Few people are incapable of doing a job properly. In my company, occasionally we have had people I thought were hopeless, but their managers have asked that they be retained and, with a bit of time and effort, they've turned them into first-class members of staff.

Managing people is difficult. It is definitely the hardest part of running a business. I've known people with a lot of professional skills or talent for commerce who have never been able to make their businesses grow. They've never been able to open more than one shop, or their professional practice has always stayed small.

The reason is that they have a problem with managing people. They will tell you it's because they cannot find people they can rely on, staff are always stealing, and so on, but the real reason is that they don't know how to motivate their employees and build a loyal and committed workforce.

Some of the excuses from employers show a lack of understanding of basic human psychology. Of course people come to take benefits for granted. You have to keep improving the incentives to keep the buzz.

When you start a new company, it's exciting for everyone and all the staff will probably be happy to put in extra hours to get the business on its feet, but as the business becomes established, the novelty wears off and you have to find new ways of maintaining that enthusiasm.

Equally, staff will not be loyal to an organisation unless it is loyal to them. Training courses and fancy Christmas parties are no substitute for basic trust between employer and employee.

It is a mistake to think there are some workplaces where staff will never be motivated.

My own industry, retail, is traditionally notorious for boring, low-paid jobs. The old stigma of 'trade' has never really disappeared in Britain, so the retail industry has suffered from a vicious circle. The jobs are poorly paid, often part time and lowly regarded. Shop assistants are assumed to be stupid by managers and customers alike, so the best and keenest people seek careers elsewhere and those that do go into retail have low expectations. Unsurprisingly, they often give the customer poor service.

At Richer Sounds we have turned this on its head. We have a waiting list for jobs in every one of our stores. Our employees are well paid, well trained and have jobs their friends envy. We aim to give good customer service and, although we don't always get it right, we think we do a better job than most because our customers come back for more.

My principles for managing and motivating people have been proved to work in my very competitive industry and they work in the wide variety of businesses to which I have been a consultant. They can apply to any kind of organisation.

The important thing is to develop a systematic and effective approach to motivating staff. Anyone can do this. You do not have to have charismatic managers or be in a glamorous industry to have a well-motivated team. There is no excuse for not getting the maximum out of your workforce.

3
The framework

If you walk into a Richer Sounds shop it will hopefully be busy and cheerful. The sales advisors will invite you to try out your own music on the latest wireless speaker, give your child a lollipop and offer to carry your purchases out to your car, having refunded the cost of your parking. They will be smiling and friendly and may even offer you a cup of coffee if they're not too busy. The whole impression we hope you will gain is that it is enjoyable to visit our shops, whether you want to leave with £1,000 of hi-fi equipment or just a free catalogue.

We think our shops are fun, both to visit and to work in, but they are also very tightly controlled places. We aim to train our shop assistants exactly how they should treat you, the customer, from the minute you enter to the minute you leave.

Good management is all about achieving the right balance between control and motivation.

Little control and lots of motivation equals anarchy. Everyone does what they want, with varying degrees of enthusiasm, but the business goes to pot.

Lots of control and no motivation means repression – you have a police state! And if there is no control and no motivation in the organisation, the result is stagnation.

So we are aiming for a highly motivated but controlled workforce.

When I say 'controlled', I don't mean treating people like slaves. Shouting at people does not mean you're controlling them. It might do something for your ego to have staff quaking at your footstep and obeying your every whim, but if the business is still losing money you have not got it right.

Control means clear standards and robust procedures. Control means there is a firm framework within which everyone works. All organisations must have rules because people must know what is expected of them. They must be expected to perform and they must know how their performance is measured. And, of course, to perform they need to be highly motivated.

Procedures are the priority

What you need are procedures that are strong enough and flexible enough to stand up to everyday use. The exact procedures will of course depend on what kind of industry or service you are in, but, as ever, the most important procedures are those that cover dealing with the customer.

At Richer Sounds we go over and over these procedures in our training. The aim is not to turn the staff into robots mouthing a script, but, where it's important, yes we do tell them exactly what to say and what not to say. For instance, they must never say to a customer, 'Can I help you?' It doesn't sound friendly and it almost always elicits the answer, 'No.' The customer then feels foolish when he or she *does* want the sale assistant's attention. And I loathe 'Are you OK there?' when a customer walks up to the till obviously requiring assistance! We leave it to individual members of staff to choose a better greeting.

These are details, but control is about getting the details right. UK companies can learn a lot from the Japanese, and Japanese companies pay great attention to details. They do not tell the employees on the production line which hand to use to assemble which parts, they tell them which finger.

Why? Because there will be one best way to perform that manoeuvre – the fastest and most efficient way – and if there is one best way then everybody should at least consider using it.

Continuous improvement

I believe passionately in continuous improvement – the Japanese principle of *kaizen* (which means 'good change'). Improvement through learning is a cornerstone of civilisation after all, and we should apply that to our organisations as well as to ourselves.

All organisations should be continually improving, which means continually looking for the best way of doing things. There is never a perfect way. Control means having a system in place to ensure that what is currently the best way is used by everyone, every time.

Central control vs. empowerment

One of the problems with talking about control is that management theorists have come up with the idea that there are broadly two ways to run a company: either with a centralised command structure or else with empowerment. Centralised control now seems to be thought of as old-fashioned, bureaucratic and inefficient, whereas empowerment is wonderful and trendy.

This is rubbish. A well-managed organisation can use both strong central control and empowerment.

Each technique has its uses and the two together should be complementary.

If you have a conglomerate of very different businesses, it is no good having the centre dictating everything, but for retailers, for example, there has to be central control because important functions like buying and marketing have to be coordinated. You wouldn't get very good deals if you had 200 stores negotiating individually with suppliers, and if you had 200 stores doing their own marketing they wouldn't be able to afford much national advertising.

So, inevitably, a lot has to be centrally organised for the sake of economies of scale, and so on. At Richer Sounds we run a very strong central structure. The reason it works is because we build in safety valves.

Too much managerial control is demotivating; our staff, an independent-minded bunch, certainly won't put up with rules they think are stupid. So we have to be aware that our central commands can never be foolproof and that there must be safety valves in terms of upwards feedback from the staff, to tell the management when commands are wrong.

Empowerment can work very well within a framework of discipline, but what people often mean by empowerment now is letting front-line employees decide how to do their jobs. I think that is dangerous, because there are usually only two ways of doing something – a right way and a wrong way – and it would be crazy not to have everyone in your organisation doing things the right way.

That does not mean there is no place for employees' own input. In my company they are empowered in two very important areas.

Freedom to serve

One area is customer satisfaction. We give staff, hopefully by training them well, complete empowerment to look after customers.

I tell the sales assistants they only need management's permission *not* to help a customer. When it comes to sorting out a customer's problem, there are no rules. If something needs putting right, or something needs doing for a customer, they have complete freedom. They do not need to ask anybody what to do and should just rely on treating the customer like a friend.

This way we can get rid of the usual excuses you hear in shops, offices and public services up and down the country: 'It's more than my job's worth', 'We can't do anything – the manager's away until next week', 'You're not allowed to do that, it's against the rules, mate'.

We train our staff to take responsibility. If a customer has a complaint the first thing the sales assistant should do is apologise, even if he or she knows nothing about the circumstances, then they can go on to sort the problem out.

Clearly, they cannot do this without a great deal of training. We can't tell them to deal with customers without giving them the tools to do the job. Empowerment is too often used by senior management as a way of palming off responsibility onto junior staff, but we believe it is management's responsibility to make sure their teams are fully equipped to cope with whatever arises. You have to develop an effective toolbox, train people how to use the tools and then allow them to get on with it.

Freedom to innovate

The other area of empowerment lies in coming up with new ideas. All staff, from the newest trainee upwards, have total freedom to come up with ideas and communicate them to management.

Many otherwise liberal companies miss out on this area of empowerment and do not give their staff the freedom to communicate.

We tell every employee that if they have an idea, they are not only empowered to tell us about it, they have a responsibility to do so.

When a new recruit joins us, the biggest item in his or her welcome pack is our *What Can We Do?* book. This is a fat book of suggestion slips ready for them to fill in, and we also have a dedicated email address for them to use if they prefer. So recruits get the message that they are expected to contribute ideas right from the start – and not just the occasional idea, but lots of them.

Freedom of views

As well as this suggestion scheme, we have many other ways staff can feed us their ideas, comments and criticisms. Each stratum of the business – sales assistants and managers – has a Colleagues' Representative, appointed to put forward their views to me or, if they prefer, the Colleagues' Council.

At our training seminars all colleagues are given the chance to discuss what questions they would like answered by the directors – a session we affectionately refer to as 'question time'. They can draw up a list of their most important concerns and if there are any the training team can't answer they will speak to someone and then get back to the colleague.

The group nominates one colleague to put the questions forward, so no one has to hold back their query for fear of being identified. As a result, the questions are very searching and can be pretty blunt. For example, at a recent session they started with, 'Are you trying to turn us in to clones? Why do we need so many standard procedures?' and went on to, 'Why have you changed the commission agreements? Do you want us to earn less?' They also asked about various other details, such as whether the uniform would be redesigned and why they weren't consulted about Boxing Day opening hours.

Sometimes there is a good answer to their questions, sometimes not. We don't always get things right and our staff are the first people to tell us so.

Your team can tell you so much of value, but only if you make it easy for them to be honest with you and if you are prepared to give an honest response. Getting people to devise questions as a group has many advantages. You are more likely to get the questions that really matter instead of trivial complaints. Individuals have personal gripes, but a concern shared by twenty people is an issue you must address.

Our message to staff is that it is their responsibility to tell us what they think. We want to improve the business continually, and we can't do so unless they tell us where we are going wrong.

Having said this, we don't like whingers. We have posters up reminding people about the Colleagues'

Representatives, Colleagues' Council, question time, the suggestion scheme, and so on, saying, 'If you have a complaint, use one of these channels to tell us about it – or else shut up!'

There are so many opportunities for people to make genuine complaints that there is no excuse for the sort of low-level moaning that can be corrosive in the workplace. People can whinge as much as they like to their families at home, but we don't want them spreading discontent among their colleagues at work.

Implementing improvements

If you have nothing but empowerment, with people free to do as they like, eventually they will conclude that managers are stupid and just not interested in either them or the job.

Managers who are interested in their business will always be looking for that continuous improvement. It sounds obvious, doesn't it? Everyone would agree organisations ought to be improving all the time, but not many businesses are. They muddle along, doing things in a certain way because they have always been done that way, or perhaps are so intent on pushing up sales that they have not paid attention to day-to-day operations.

33

To achieve continuous improvement, first of all you have to think of the improvements that could be made. If your reaction is, 'There aren't any', you are bound to be wrong! Second, once you have developed improvements, you have to make sure they are implemented throughout the organisation.

Empowerment can produce some real creative thinking, but although there might be a thousand good new initiatives across the whole company, there is no continuous improvement if it's all done locally.

In a company where overall control is weak, you will get a branch coming up with a good idea. The branch manager tells the area manager about it, and the area manager buries it because they do not want other areas they are competing with to copy it. Or perhaps one department develops good practice, but rivalry prevents them from sharing it with any other departments, so initiatives fizzle out.

It depends whether you really believe in improvement. We believe that there's only one best way to do most things (until we improve on it) so we like to impose that best way globally. The trick here is not to make it too regimented. The things you make compulsory are things that have to be compulsory. If a rule isn't really necessary, strip it away.

That has to be the continual process. You have to keep looking to make sure you are not sending so many instructions to staff that they can't budge for rules and regulations.

We aim for a balance. We want to hear about initiatives and, when we adopt them, everyone has to adopt them, but they are only fixed in stone until a better idea comes along. At the same time, there are only a certain number of hours in the day and we don't want to set down so many onerous restrictions that people can't get on with their jobs.

Once again, we get staff to tell us when the rules are too restrictive. We constantly look at our procedures and paperwork to make sure the systems are not clogged up with requirements that are unreasonable, duplicated or no longer needed. We believe in streamlining wherever possible.

Ideas and more ideas

A healthy organisation feeds on ideas, suggestions, comments and criticisms. I carry memo cards with me everywhere to jot down my own ideas and what people say to me – in meetings, in the stores, when I'm travelling.

However, the most important engine in the drive for improvement in Richer Sounds is not me or senior management, but my colleagues. Several years ago when Ideas UK looked at the number of suggestions per colleague we generated (around twenty), we had the highest number per employee of any organisation in the UK. Of all the statistics about the company, this is the one that gives me the most satisfaction.

Many companies have suggestion schemes and others have different quality initiatives – quality circles, Total Quality Management, and so on. They are just various names for institutionalising or systemising the improvement of the business.

Before I introduced the suggestion scheme at Richer Sounds, I probably used to come up with 90 per cent of the ideas for improving the company and that was hard work. It felt like pushing a wagon uphill. Now 90 per cent of the suggestions come from the staff and I am sitting on the wagon, being pulled up that hill.

A good suggestion scheme is like having an oil well in your back garden. There is no more valuable tool for management.

We invite customers to send us their comments too, but very often they are not commercially practical. Only 1 per cent of customer ideas can be taken up, whereas 20 per cent of our staff suggestions are worthy of further consideration. In terms of the time allocated to them, you will get more practical value from staff panels than customer panels.

This is not to say that talking to your customers is not important. Instead, we ask customers how they feel we have let them down, rather than how can we run our business better. As part of our customer service drive, we try to generate as many customer responses as possible, because you cannot improve service unless you know what you are doing wrong.

I have often met senior managers who say their company tried to introduce a suggestion scheme but it didn't take off. There are usually good reasons why their schemes didn't work. Our Richer Sounds scheme works extraordinarily well and is the cornerstone of *kaizen* in our business. I can guarantee that the principles of our scheme will work for any organisation.

How to run an effective suggestion scheme

1. The most senior person in the organisation must be involved with the scheme

That person is supposed to be the wisest and most experienced person in the business and their involvement will give the scheme credibility. They also have a global view of the company and – most importantly – they have the power to ensure that good ideas are actually implemented.

I always recommend the chair or chief executive of the organisation as the figurehead and that has been a big factor in the success of these schemes.

Even when I have advised very large companies, I have stressed that the top person must be involved in the scheme. It is certainly a job that I personally would never delegate to someone else.

It does not have to be a time-consuming chore. The chief executive will not have to see every suggestion, only the new ideas. An efficient department will do the job of sifting and allocating the suggestions, preparing responses, and so on. However, if the chief executive signs the letter, thanking the member of staff for his or her suggestion, the impact on morale will be tremendous.

2. Make it easy for people to enter their suggestions

Do not create obstacles with complicated eight-page forms to fill in with their life story.

Our *What Can We Do?* book is very simple and everyone has one. For us, they can send in a suggestion written on a serviette in a restaurant and as long as we can read it, we don't care.

3. Answer all the suggestions

There is nothing more soul-destroying than to put in a suggestion and never hear about it. As well as it being common courtesy to acknowledge when people have taken the trouble to send in an idea, staff will feel recognised and encouraged. Everyone who puts in a suggestion to our scheme receives a handwritten note from me or a senior director. Whether the idea is finally used or not, each person feels they have contributed.

4. Answer suggestions quickly

I have heard horrendous stories of major UK companies being as much as eighteen months behind in evaluating suggestions. If there is ever a disincentive for putting in suggestions, it must be the knowledge that you could wait eighteen months before your suggestion is even considered.

5. Encourage people to meet in small groups

It is difficult to come up with suggestions on your own, but when you are sitting in the pub with your mates after work, the ideas flow thick and fast.

6. Reward little and often

A lot of company schemes go wrong by rewarding only those suggestions that save money. The arrangement is usually some sort of percentage of the savings that result, but good ideas are not just about saving money. One example was a suggestion from a shop manager that we should install doorbells at wheelchair height for disabled customers who might have difficulty in getting through the doors. Needless to say, this *didn't* save us any money – in fact, it cost us to fit all the bells – but it *was* a useful contribution to customer service.

We want good customer service, so that is what we reward. We start by giving a small cash prize for every suggestion we receive, provided it isn't abusive or something staff are supposed to be doing anyway. Colleagues can be rewarded a maximum of £25, because motivational rewards up to that amount are tax-free.

Because the prizes are small and there are no complex criteria to assess, we can award them immediately. It does not matter if the suggestion is a duplicate or if we have thought of it before and not implemented it for technical reasons, they still get something by way of thanks.

At Richer Sounds we find that around one in five ideas are worthy of further consideration. We only measure how many get to this stage, rather than saying how many are implemented, because by the time the initiative is rolled out – after design, costing, trial, and so on – it could be months or years after the suggestion was made and the idea could have changed out of all recognition.

Every quarter I pick out the two best suggestions for an extra prize. The winners can choose from a menu of different prizes, such as a weekend at a health farm or a trip on the *Orient Express*.

Our reward scheme does not cause resentment because we have lots and lots of winners. Nearly everybody gets a prize, even if it's only £5. Meanwhile, the company is not wasting time and money having teams of evaluators working out the savings.

In some very big companies, a good suggestion could save perhaps £100,000. The reward might be 10 per cent of the savings, but if someone wins £10,000 you find their colleagues are resentful, while the winner is also grumbling because they think it should have been £12,000. And the person working next to them might have had a brilliant idea, but was not rewarded because it didn't save the company money.

7. Measure and publish the results

On our monthly report to colleagues we list the number of suggestions received from each department or branch and the money they have earnt for the year to date.

This creates powerful peer pressure. When one shop sees they have only put in twenty suggestions this year and others have put in fifty, they call an ideas meeting very quickly.

8. Use the ideas

It sounds obvious, but for a scheme to have ultimate credibility, you must put the ideas into practice. That is the way improvements are made.

I once asked a group of employees how many of them had put in a suggestion that had been used and forty out of fifty people put up their hands. That means 80 per cent knew they had made an input into the company and had really contributed to its development. That is very motivating.

This is why we can have a tightly controlled system: because people don't feel they are just the passive recipients of endless orders. Not only can they question and criticise, but they also know that many of the rules are based on their own ideas for improvements, taken up and put into practice for everyone.

There will always be things that people do not like doing, but if they can see it is for the good of the business, they will accept the constrictions.

Carrots and sticks

To impose control, you need the stick and the carrot. Most organisations do not offer much in the way of carrots, although some are heavy-handed with the stick. At Richer Sounds we have lovely juicy carrots to get people motivated. We also have a very big stick, but most of the time we keep it hidden. For a stick to be effective you don't have to use it often – it will be effective as long as people know it's there and that you will use it without hesitation if necessary.

I like having lots of carrots, but if there are rewards and no penalties then your staff will think you're a soft touch. I am not a believer in self-regulation; I don't think many people would pay income tax if we didn't have tax inspectors.

Some companies use fines for small-scale problems, for instance when people have been careless or persistently unpunctual. I prefer to use fines as little as possible and have found that one of the most effective penalties is publicity. When I do my weekly taped broadcast for all the colleagues telling them the latest news, I will mention by name anyone (from management only) who has done something particularly stupid – people are not crazy about being singled out in this way for the whole company to hear. It's a powerful deterrent.

Every company has to decide its own balance between carrot and stick. At Richer Sounds we only bring the stick out in extreme circumstances and, for us, the worst crime is theft. Integrity is the core of our culture so we show no mercy to staff who cheat us. We make sure there can be no excuse for stealing, because anyone in real financial straits only has to turn to our Helping Hand fund (we put 1 per cent of profits into a Helping Hand hardship fund to provide grants or interest-free loans for staff use).

We also point out that since over 30 per cent of our profits go on staff bonuses or to charity, around a third of what they take is stolen from their colleagues or from good causes. So theft means dismissal and not only do we not give in and write a nice reference afterwards, we might even go to the trouble of ringing up a subsequent employer to ask if they know that that person was kicked out for stealing.

Staff do not object to these tough sanctions as long as they know the rules are applied in full and applied consistently. Respect for the rules would break down if people thought that some offenders were getting away with being dishonest while others were punished.

Measuring performance

If you are making improvements, you want them implemented consistently throughout the organisation. This is why it is essential to measure performance constantly.

We make sure that our staff's performance is fed back to them all the time. This is done through weekly measures, which set out each shop's or department's performance the previous week, measured against a range of criteria.

Obviously we measure sales, but we also measure the date of the oldest repair that needs doing for a customer, how many repairs are outstanding, how many staff worked a six-day week, their customer service results, and so on. Every Monday morning the two directors of the operations and sales teams each host conference calls with all stores to discuss any issues and go through their figures with them.

Measuring performance is only part of the process of making sure that people in your organisation do what you want them to do. The other way to get results is through reward, as I will explain in the next chapter. Napoleon wanted brave generals, so it's no surprise that he rewarded bravery. If you want staff to give great customer service or increase profits, you have to reward those things, as well as measure them.

The Richer Way League

Every month branches, central support departments and the warehouse are measured on their performance. For the shops, sales and customer service are obviously important measures. We also count positive things, such as their monthly branch visit scores, as well as negative things, such as absenteeism.

All this is valuable management information; it also shows the stores exactly how they are doing and where there is room for improvement. We know everyone has good and bad weeks, but we must also see quickly if a branch is in difficulties and do something about it. A commitment to continuous improvement means you cannot ignore under-performance: if there has been a bad week, you must tackle the problems immediately, before performance really goes into decline.

Our Birmingham branch, for instance, had to struggle for a whole year with the road in front of the shop being dug up. It was a deterrent to customers and sales went down, but the performance sheets showed the staff compensated by working so hard at customer satisfaction that the quality of their sales went up. They made fewer sales, but by the end of the year they had made higher profits than the year before.

League tables and prizes are one way of motivating people, but they are not the only way. We are aiming for highly motivated people and we go about creating that motivation in a completely comprehensive way.

4

The fun – generating and measuring motivation

What motivates people to put in a good day's work? Money? Fear of unemployment? Loyalty? Professional pride?

Of course there are many factors motivating all of us, usually a mixture of the positive – such as reward and recognition – and the negative – such as penalties and failure. Most employers understand about the penalties, but often they do not think of harnessing the positive factors. The only carrot they know about is pay, which is a fairly crude tool for motivating people.

However, it is possible to create in your organisation the positive factors for motivating people. Every member of staff is different and will respond in different ways, but, taken together, the following five steps form a programme that will raise the levels of motivation throughout the workforce.

Five steps to motivating people

1. Fun

Start with fun. You don't need a Ph.D. in psychology to know that if you enjoy what you do, you do it better. If you're being treated nastily at work you do not enjoy it, so you do the minimum, take days off sick and go home early. It is amazing how many companies appear not to understand this. At Richer Sounds we aim to treat all our staff decently and we pay them the living wage.[†] On top of that, we have a lot of extras that make the job fun.

Holiday time

We have ten holiday homes around the country with two more recently acquired in Venice and Paris. Any of our colleagues, together with their families and friends (and pets), can use the holiday homes for free depending only on length of service and not seniority (although we do ask for a small contribution towards the benefit-in-kind tax the company pays for the colleague on this).

I remember my bank manager at the time saying to me, most politely, that I was crazy when I asked to borrow the money to buy the first home.

† As defined by the Living Wage Foundation and *not* to be compared with the lower national minimum wage.

He agreed the loan, but said we did not need to do this. Exactly – the reason I provide holiday homes is because I don't need to. I give people more than I need to and I get more in return.

I always make it clear to staff that the holiday homes are not part of their salary package. Cynics might say we provide these goodies so we can pay our employees less, but that is not so. All our salaries are at the top end of the market rates for the job they apply to. We think it is important not to trade off perks against salaries – otherwise they are not perks.

Is this paternalistic and patronising? I don't think so, because the real test is whether staff actually use the holiday homes. They do: the homes are booked for hundreds of nights a year. People take their friends and families along and we find the homes are not abused.

There is a sound logic too behind providing holiday homes. We want relaxed, happy, healthy staff. Very many of them grew up and live in urban areas, and do not have easy access to the countryside or the sea, so the holiday homes make a refreshing change to their normal environment.

Like most companies, we have employees strapped with heavy mortgages and houses going down in value, but there's no reason now for them not to have a holiday – or indeed several good holidays a year in different locations.

There are lots of other things a company can do to make work fun. As well as social events after hours, there can be competitions within work to spice it up a little.

Benefits and incentives

New people joining us receive our *Benefits and Incentives* booklet, which sets out all the rewards they can earn and the entitlements they qualify for while working for Richer Sounds. It is a very attractive list. It includes substantial benefits, such as our private healthcare scheme and, of course, discounts on TV and hi-fi equipment. There is also a range of other rewards for good ideas so, for instance, a colleague who finds a new location for a store would be substantially rewarded if the location were acquired.

I try to avoid setting dangerous precedents, however. One branch manager came to me with a proposal for a deal with a local health club: free membership for colleagues in his store in return for discounts on our hi-fis. I had to turn the idea down because I felt it would not be fair on the other shops, which did not have this perk. It would create resentment. Sometimes you have to be firm to be fair and, when it comes to perks, it is best to keep special cases to a minimum. People remember anomalies and you find they can be thrown back at you years later.

Training

In many companies, junior staff do not even know what the chairman looks like. At Richer Sounds, staff start off their careers with a four-day training course in our Stockport office followed by three days in London. This includes a session with me, where I talk to them about Richer Sounds and welcome them into the company. This helps create loyalty and trust from the outset.

In addition to spending time each morning learning about the products we sell, prior to the store opening, we also have an annual seminar for our store managers and deputy managers (or DMs), which includes training sessions with many of our suppliers. We also like to make these two-day meetings as much fun as possible so in the evening we have a party, music courtesy of a band made up of several colleagues, with me on drums. Everyone seems to have a lot of fun and some spend the night partying, but we do not care as long as they are up for their first session the next day.

Workaholics are no fun

There is another, very important, side to having fun. All the Bentleys in the world won't make a job fun if people are working long hours and becoming exhausted. I don't provide holiday homes and then expect people to work seven days a week.

No one can work well and be truly motivated if they are run down, but so many people these days, in all sorts of workplaces, put in very long hours. This is a problem, not something to be proud of. It is an employer's responsibility to make sure staff only work so many hours and don't run themselves into the ground. People must have time for their families and be allowed a social life.

The only way to tackle this is for the chief executive to lay down clearly that people are expected to just work their hours, and no more. If you don't spell it out, people will assume they have to work longer and longer.

There are four reasons why people might work long hours. First, there are the ones who live for their job. They love their work, they have no social life, no family, and they never seem to go home. That's all very well if they enjoy the job and they are certainly valuable members of staff, but somebody still has to stand over them and say, 'Hang on, you've worked sixty hours this week – this has got to stop.'

Work fanatics worry me. I literally have to force them to go home sometimes. They must be made to take a break, for their own sakes and the sake of their work, because their output is much better when they're refreshed.

The manager must control this problem by knowing how many hours each person is working.

At Richer Sounds it is part of our culture that we have a five-day week and people only work six-day weeks or overtime if there is an exceptional reason for it.

I am strict about this because a few years ago I lost the manager of one of our branches through not being aware of how hard he had been working. He walked out over an apparently trivial criticism and refused to come back. It was not until afterwards that I discovered he had been working six or seven days a week for months and had understandably become exhausted and resentful.

I vowed this would not happen again, so now each shop and department has to record how many hours and days each staff member worked. If people are working six days a week an explanation must be provided.

The second reason for long hours might be that people simply cannot fit their workload into a normal working day. Perhaps management has piled more and more tasks on to them and they are trying to fit twelve hours' work into a day.

So if people are working late, is it because you are short-staffed? Managers must find out whether they are asking people to do too much. This is not always easy because you get people doing apparently similar jobs, one of whom seems to handle it easily, the other always complaining there is too much work.

The way to tackle this is with a kind of time and motion study. Pick someone who is a good worker, but not exceptional, and see how they get on with that task. If they cannot do the work in the time allowed, you know you have to increase their resources and get help for them.

If they can cope, but others can't, you may need to help those under pressure organise their time better.

Some people cannot manage their time. I've seen people working in the office until 8 p.m., but I know they're the ones who will be on the phone for half an hour when a five-minute conversation would do, or the ones who are nipping out for a fag break every half-hour. They look like martyrs, working late into the night, but if they had got down to their job during the day they could have done it all and left work on the dot at five.

These people need training in time management. They can be helped to become more disciplined and use their time more effectively.

The worst cause of long hours is the macho culture. This is a corrosive problem in the workplace and one which senior management needs to deal with firmly. The macho culture rules when someone working in an open-plan office finishes their work by 4.30 p.m. on a nice sunny day, looks out of the window and sees the car park is full. They dare not get up and leave because as they walk across that office twenty people will look up and say, 'Oh, half-day, John?' So everyone sticks it out, pretending to work, because no one dares to be the first to go home.

This is ridiculous. In my company support offices, I want people to be proud that on a nice afternoon they can get their work finished and go to the park. In summer, when our shops are quieter, we don't object to managers working a four-day week if they can organise themselves effectively and the shop is performing well. As long as they are there for the busy periods and they are confident their staff can manage without them, we leave it up to them to decide how to use their time.

These rules have to come down from the top, though. The macho culture arises because, unless they're told otherwise, people assume when they get a job that the harder they work the better they'll get on. When I ask managers if they want their staff to work such long hours, they usually say no. Unless management sends out the positive message that staff must not work long hours, the assumption is that it is expected.

The mistake is to equate working long hours with working hard. The fault of many managers is that they don't know how well their staff are working. They couldn't tell you whether that person was doing a good job or not – the only thing they see is how long someone spends at their desk. That is a really prehistoric way of managing. What managers should have is a proper measuring system in place to assess people's effectiveness.

It is different, of course, for chief executives, who can't expect to stick to an eight-hour day, but they have chosen that lifestyle and they are normally highly paid for it. Their burnout rate may be higher, but so are the rewards. That doesn't mean that all their employees have to burn themselves out for £20,000 a year.

Long hours are rarely quality time. People are not working at their best when they are tired. They get stressed out and many become ill. Their relationships at home will suffer. They also become stale and lose their enthusiasm and creativity. You may squeeze a few extra hours out of them each week, but if they have to take two weeks off sick twice a year, you have gained nothing.

So if you take charge of hours worked and cut down on people working late into the evening and at weekends, you will find the payback is good. In the end, you will see that long hours drive the good people away (they will come to work for companies like ours where they know they will work a five-day week).

Stress control

Senior managers like to talk about all the stress they suffer, but employers must remember that work is usually more stressful for their staff than for them. Stress is largely caused by not having control of your own destiny.

I have a relatively stress-free existence: I start work when I want and I have time off when I want. I have various business crises to deal with, but that is quite a different sort of stress from getting to work on time and putting up with your boss's tantrums.

Stress is not only due to long hours and too much work. It is also caused by lack of communication. People become stressed when managers do not tell them what is going on, impose decisions that don't seem to make any sense and do not allow staff any reply. One of your first tasks if you want to reduce levels of stress in your organisation is to improve your communication – both downwards and upwards.

The fun is real

You might be thinking that it's all very well for me to say my staff have fun, but how can I be so sure? The answer is that we ask them in our staff attitude survey (see appendices A and B), which we do every year. This is conducted anonymously so they can be completely frank. In the latest survey, 86 per cent of our support department colleagues and 91 per cent of our store colleagues said it was fun working for Richer Sounds.

Every month the winning branch in our inter-branch competition wins the use of a beautiful Bentley Arnage, complete with the unique number plate LUN1E. The car is theirs to use for the month as they wish and we even pay for the petrol! I don't ask them what they get up to in the car, but I know they have a lot of fun!

You can't order people to enjoy themselves. And we realise that however hard you try, your people aren't going to be happy all the time, but you can create the right working environment in which they can have fun and you can try different ideas to see what people like. Many of our initiatives have actually been suggested by our colleagues.

2. Recognition

How often do you say to your staff, 'Well done and thank you'? It's the cheapest, most effective way of motivating people and it's the one we do worst.

When did you last write a letter saying thank you? When did you last reward people in recognition of achievement? Perhaps you remember to say thank you when you have the time, or someone has done something exceptional, but most employers would admit that a lot of good work goes unrecognised.

The answer is to build recognition into your systems. I am amazed how few organisations do this.

It is certainly the quickest fix I can recommend to start motivating people.

Letters can be a chore, but it's important to do them, and do them straight away. When I visit a store and it looks good, I always drop them a line afterwards to say so. I've seen these letters pinned on stockroom noticeboards two years later, still a source of pride.

It is essential to be consistent with recognition. Spontaneous gestures of appreciation are nice, but there is a danger that some members of staff will be treated more favourably than others. Make sure it is not only the extroverts who get recognised.

Apart from being liberal with the thank-you letters, flowers and boxes of chocolates, you can introduce recognition schemes. For instance, at Richer Sounds we hand out gold aeroplane badges for our 'high-flyers' – people who have performed above and beyond the call of duty, perhaps by giving exceptional customer service or having a really brilliant idea.

This is only a badge, but it is a visible sign of recognition. The really clever thing is that we advertise it in our catalogue, telling customers to look out for our staff wearing gold aeroplanes. They feel proud to wear the badge and it often sparks a conversation when customers ask how they earnt it.

The point about recognition is that it must be part of the culture of the organisation. It is no good expecting people to work late night after night and then think they can be mollified with a bunch of flowers. These letters and gold aeroplanes are gestures that cost very little, but they have their place alongside a whole basket of other measures.

I got annoyed when companies I advised as a consultant said, 'Oh, we could do the badges. That won't cost us much.' They have not understood that a few badges won't change the culture. If a gold aeroplane is just a way to avoid giving employees a decent pay rise, it doesn't mean a thing.

I always make a point of phoning our branches. Of course, a lot of managing directors do that, but they only phone the ten worst branches to give them a rocket. That's the wrong approach. When a branch or department has had a bad week, they know it very well and are dreading that phone call. If you do phone, it should be to give some support and find out what went wrong.

In our Monday-morning phone calls to the stores, if the branch has had a bad week they get a shoulder to cry on (obviously if the figures are poor consistently there may be a bigger problem), and if they've done well they get a pat on the back. I also mention on my weekly message all the best performing stores to say a big well done and I phone every manager every month when their management accounts are published.

In my company we're quick to criticise mistakes, but we're also quick to praise. We do try to criticise in a positive way and to learn continually from mistakes.

Management by walking around

Most managers know how important it is to walk around their office or factory and talk to people – but how often do they do it? Unless it is in your diary and you make it part of your routine, it won't happen.

Although I'm not in the office that often, I do pop into the central support departments to say hello to people when I am. In addition, if I'm near any of my branches during my travels I will always drop in. I ask three questions: is everything OK? Is there anything you want to tell me? Is there anything you need help with?

One of our most junior warehouse colleagues was once asked what he liked most about working for Richer Sounds. He said, 'It's that I can talk to the owner.' People can see I care about what's going on and I'm interested in them. And that's even more important than the holiday homes.

The Five-Year Club

It is important that recognition doesn't only go to the high-flyers. In any organisation there are a lot of people who will never be managers, and don't want to be. They are the backbone of the business, but they are often neglected.

I was concerned about this in my company. As we have matured and grown, there are increasing numbers of employees who have put in years of good service, but are not rising up the management tree and are not therefore getting attention from the board.

So we have set up the Five-Year Club. After five years' service, colleagues get a sterling-silver lapel pin and I take them all on a holiday every year thereafter. Holidays in the past have involved youth hostelling, hiking, camping, etc., but recently they have included trips to Amsterdam, Barcelona, Paris, Berlin, Venice, Whitby and Brighton. I enjoy these holidays a lot – our Five-Year Club people are a down-to-earth bunch and not afraid to enjoy themselves. Nor are they afraid to be outspoken about life in the branches, so I get a good picture of what is happening at the front line.

We also give our colleagues a ten-year gift. It is not the traditional gold watch because most people already have a watch by the time they're thirty-five. Instead, we give them £500 to spend on a present of their choice.

Finally, everyone in the company gets a bit of extra recognition on their birthday. They get the day off, they receive a birthday card from me and we will pay for a cake that they can share with colleagues and customers. This idea, like so many, was a staff suggestion.

3. Rewards

Most businesses want their employees to give good service, but they don't reward them for it. Instead, they base rewards solely on profit, turnover or market share.

If you want your staff to give great service, then reward them for great service. It sounds easy, but so many organisations get this completely wrong.

If we look at motivation through reward, I believe flat salaries by themselves are very demotivating. However high the salary is, if you're not being rewarded for doing better, it is only human for your performance to slacken off in time.

I learnt a lesson many years ago from a shop I had a joint share in. The manager opted for flat salaries and he paid good money, but within a few months we found staff were stealing. We asked why, since they were paid well, and they said that they were bored because however much better they did at the job they didn't get any further reward.

It was a pathetic reason, but it's a fact of life that some people think like that and you must not give them that excuse.

Plenty of winners

The most important thing about rewards is to have lots of winners. It is much more motivating for lots of people to win small prizes, so that everyone knows they are in with a chance of winning, than for a small number of people to win big prizes, causing resentment among the rest of the staff.

Again, I find 90 per cent of organisations fall flat on that score. I've seen companies that have, say, a Branch of the Year award for their 300 shops. Of those 300 shops, at least 200 will work really hard for that award.

The prize might be a car but there's only one winner so 199 stores are left feeling resentful and the top fifty are angry, swearing that that's the last time they ever get involved in a competition. Typically also, the winning manager cannot drive or has already got a better model.

It is always better to give 1,000 people £10, than one person £10,000. After all, the margin between the winners and the losers is usually small and there's always an element of luck.

Reward schemes must be kept simple. To have a fair reward scheme, there first has to be a good system of performance measurement. Again, some companies say this causes resentment and suspicion, but in my experience people don't mind being measured as long as they understand:

A. Why they are measured. Make it clear, for in-
    stance, that you are measuring customer ser-
    vice in order to improve it.
B. How they are measured. People want to under-
    stand the rules and the rules must be logical,
    sensible and fair. Some organisations' schemes
    are ridiculously complicated and seem unfair,
    so people start juggling their figures to match
    the scheme. Staff must also have the opportu-
    nity to make an input to the scheme and get
    unfair rules changed.
C. That they will be rewarded for good per-
    formance.

A good example is the mystery shopper scheme,
which we use to measure customer service. Many
companies use it, but unless the scheme is handled
well it can create ill feeling among staff, who think
they may be criticised unfairly.

A scheme whereby employees can be penalised or
rewarded on the word of an anonymous person does
run the risk of being unpopular, so we have introduced a £100 jackpot for any member of staff who
achieves a high score on the mystery shopper report.
My staff now can't wait (almost!) for them to turn up.

How to reward
You can reward any aspect of your work you want.
Businesses often say they want their staff to give

good service but they cannot reward it because it is too subjective and can't be assessed. They are wrong – you can reward anything if you take the trouble to measure it properly. It takes more effort, but it can be done.

True, good service is subjective. The only measure that counts is whether the customer feels the service has been satisfactory. So we ask them. On our receipts we have a very short form for customers to return, saying what they thought of the service. Every time the customer ticks 'excellent', that sales assistant receives a £5 bonus.

This does mean a customer can come in, spend £5, be delighted with the service and the salesperson gets £5. In effect, we've paid out 100 per cent of the sale price. The accountants would have me carried off by the men in the white coats for such a crazy scheme, but I know that a customer who buys a few batteries today may be back for a hi-fi tomorrow. Customer service has to be for every customer.

The other side of the coin, of course, is that if the customer says service was poor, the salesperson is fined £5. If a colleague is mentioned by name in a complimentary letter they receive a payment of up to £20 for good comments, however a colleague mentioned by name for poor service could be fined as much as £10. As I've said, you need sticks as well as carrots. If this sounds punitive, we do

not actually make deductions from pay if someone has a minus figure for this scheme at the end
of the month, but they might have some explain-
ing to do as to why they should still have a job
with us.

We find the mystery shopper scheme very useful as an objective measure of customer service.
Mystery shopper personnel visit shops anonymously and report on the service they receive.
These reports are very detailed, covering whether
the shopper was greeted on entering the store,
whether they were offered a catalogue, and so on.
We publish these reports internally and they make
up part of our performance measurement.

As our sales advisors wear name badges, the report specifically comments on individual members
of the shop team. You sometimes hear criticism
that it is unfair to single out colleagues by name,
but I disagree: unless the person who gave bad service is identified, the entire shop could be tarred
with the same brush. However, I made a promise
that when I read out the results on our weekly tape
that I won't identify the person involved unless it
is management.

As well as having several levels of reward, it
is also best to have several reward schemes. It is
more interesting and more fun. People think, 'OK,
I didn't do so well on that competition but I've got
a chance with this one.'

You should try to reward as many people in the organisation as possible. We do this by giving all central departments a share of the total profit made at the end of each financial year. After all, in a sales-orientated business like mine, why should secretaries and warehouse staff lose out just because they do not talk directly to the customer?

What about other kinds of reward? Having given up myself, I decided it would be nice to reward people for stopping smoking. It seemed contradictory that although the company is against smoking, we end up rewarding smokers because they tend to take more breaks so they can have a cigarette, and that annoys the non-smokers. To try to discourage this behaviour we give a £300 reward to any colleague who stops smoking for a year. When they notify us of their intention to stop they receive a dated 'I give up' certificate and if they manage to stop smoking for a year the certificate is returned to us for redemption – so if they are weak-willed their first cigarette will cost them £300! I give directors £1,500 because their time is more expensive.

Very many people have taken me up on this and I've written a lot of cheques. I don't check up on whether they have smoked or not: if I can't trust them then they shouldn't be working for me.

Profit sharing

Profit share is a very important part of the rewards package. Everybody who works for Richer Sounds receives a share of the profits of the company in some form.

All managers, deputy managers and acting managers working in a branch receive a contribution bonus, which is based on the contribution their store makes towards the profit of the company.

Each branch contribution is calculated on a monthly basis from its sales, margin, variable costs and an estimate of its fixed costs. From this, a bonus is calculated for each level of seniority within the branch and the frequency of this bonus creates a major spur to the colleagues, who can see each sale the branch makes being converted into cash for them.

Receiving profit share little and often is good motivation and people feel involved in the company's performance. Colleagues regard it as genuinely extra and not part of their salary.

At the end of each year, after the branch stocktakes have been completed, an accounting reconciliation is performed and if the store has performed over target an extra bonus is then paid out.

Accordingly, they receive a bonus once a year calculated from the profits of the company as a whole. We don't have a complex hierarchy of reward. There are three different levels of profit share – for non-managers, managers and the board directors. These are three quite different areas of responsibility within the company, and everyone at each level (excluding directors) receives the same share.

Pay and commission

We don't pay staff extra for length of service or academic qualifications. We pay purely on their ability to do their job.

Our overall policy is to pay at the top level of the market rate for the jobs people do within our section of the retail industry. We keep an eye on what our competitors are doing and are confident that we pay the best.

When there is a new venture or a new type of job behind the scenes for which there might be little evidence of the market rate, I make a point of asking the person concerned how much they think they should be paid for that job. If they are not sure I ask them to base their figure on what they think the market rate is, what their peers are earning, how much they need to live on reasonably and what salary level they would be happy with.

Sales commission is never based on hitting turnover targets. Turnover too often conflicts with customer service. If a customer comes into the shop wanting to spend £300 and you persuade them to part with £500, what kind of service is that? If you are serious about service, staff should always earn more from giving good customer service than from pushing through a sale.

We do pay commission, but not pro rata to sales. This is much fairer, and more productive than the target bonus schemes other companies run. Firms will often tell their salesforce they can earn so much if they hit a set target for a certain period. This leads to distortions: salespeople don't bother to work much one month then they try to cram all the deals into another month in order to hit the target. Then again, if someone reaches 95 per cent of their target they don't get a bean. It is much better to pay proportional commission.

Sales commission is in fact not the most important addition to our employees' pay. In general, the larger proportion of a staff member's salary is earnt through various customer service bonuses, profit sharing and other incentives such as the suggestion scheme.

The low basic salary can be off-putting to job applicants and a problem for staff trying to take out a mortgage or a loan. We get round this by guaranteeing the living wage as a minimum to everyone who joins us, after three months' service.

The company has also negotiated an agreement with Barclays Bank ensuring that staff can count their bonuses as part of their salary when getting a mortgage with Barclays.

Any company that uses commission schemes will have to revise them from time to time. It is best to explain to staff when they are recruited that the commission scheme will change, to avoid confusion and resentment among the sales team when you have to do this.

4. Communication

You cannot motivate a workforce if you don't communicate with them.

A big part of motivation is about having a two-way, continuous dialogue between you and your employees. You cannot motivate people unless you tell them what is going on and in turn listen to what they've got to say.

I don't just mean issuing instructions. Downward communication should be both informative and instructive. These are two different things. Many companies are very good at doing the instructive communication, i.e. laying down the rules – do this, do that, be in the office by nine o'clock, and so on.

Another very important part of downward communication is information, such as telling people how well the organisation is doing, how it can do better and what the strategy is. It is this communication that is an important component in creating good morale. At Richer Sounds we do this through the finance packs, my monthly phone calls to every manager, constructive store visits, my weekly tapes, and so on. Our seminars are also an invaluable part of informative downwards communication – I aim to send everyone away buzzing with enthusiasm.

That is top-down communication. Upwards communication is listening to people's ideas, views and problems, through such systems as Colleagues' Representatives, question time, suggestion schemes and career counselling.

There must also be sideways communication. Make sure that branches and departments are encouraged to have a dialogue and support each other. We encourage people from the central support departments, like accounts and marketing, to go and work in the stores, to make sure they understand the problems there. All directors must experience working on the shop floor, if only for a couple of days a year. People from the stores also come and work in the central support departments at Richer House. All central support departments' vacancies are advertised initially to the branches.

In many businesses, the people at headquarters have the glamorous jobs, the personal parking spaces and the directors' dining room. It creates a huge gulf between front-line staff and the people at the top.

In my company, the branches are the heroes and the central departments work incredibly hard to support them. We don't call Richer House 'head office' because that implies it is more important than the branches, when the reverse is true.

It is good that the branches don't see jobs at Richer House as cushy. When colleagues do come to work at one of the central support departments, for instance joining the marketing team, we always guarantee them their old job back if the pressure gets too much for them. If someone chooses to go back to their branch after a while then that is not regarded as failure.

An element of communication that should not be forgotten is how important it is for managers to admit mistakes. When bosses pretend to be perfect they are fooling no one but themselves. Staff find out when you have made mistakes and if you own up to it, you will regain their respect. Senior managers often think that leading from the front means they must appear to be infallible, but it is much better to admit you are human. I have found that when I have made mistakes and acknowledged them to the rest of the company, I have far more credibility than if I had tried to cover them up.

Ways to communicate

Rather than sending out reams of memos and emails, I communicate directly with the branches via recorded message every week. It is the next best thing to face-to-face. We go for the cheap, easy-access approach – I record a message every Sunday and the colleagues either call in on a Monday morning to pick it up or listen online.

I tell them how we did the previous week, share the latest news and include important messages I want to get across.

Of course, we then have to check that they have heard it. I include a code word at the end of the message, which they have to tell the ops team on their Monday-morning call so we can be hopeful that they have listened to it.

We only send an email out to all branches once a week or to alert them to a safety issue. The more emails you send, the less people read them. If central departments resort to lots of emails to all branches, we take that as a sign they are not very well organised.

I also make a point of visiting every branch and talking to the teams in detail. This is their opportunity to tell me about their concerns and if they have a problem I can sort it out when I get back to the office. It is an invaluable exercise because people tell you so much more in a face-to-face chat. When I am able to fix their problems this also sends a powerful message that I take an interest in everyone who works for the company.

It is a huge investment of my time, and it is hard work, but it is an invaluable way for me to find out what is really happening there.

Seminars and training are all good forms of communication, as are my rounds of central support departments and the warehouse.

Communication starts the minute people join us. All new recruits receive a welcome pack, telling them all about the company and their job. I am always present at our Virgin Seminars for new recruits, to welcome them and communicate directly with them.

The first thing new employees do on joining a shop is to learn our mission statement, which is called *The Richer Way*. This is simply three principles:

- To provide second-to-none service and value for money for our customers.
- To provide ourselves with secure, well-paid jobs, working in a stimulating, equal-opportunities environment.
- To be profitable to ensure our long-term growth and survival.

So motivation for the new recruit starts on day one.

5. Loyalty

Most companies expect loyalty from their staff but they do not show much loyalty in return.

Richer Sounds has a range of measures by which we show staff that we value them and will stand by them in their difficulties. For a start, there is our Helping Hand hardship fund, which provides grants or interest-free loans to staff who are struggling financially.

This is money to help them, or indeed any member of their family. Maybe their partner has been made redundant and they have sudden financial difficulties. We are not judgemental. In fact, as I said earlier, the fund is partly there as a safety valve to prevent theft. We want our staff to know that whatever trouble they are in, they don't have to steal.

There are certain things the hardship fund is not for. We don't dish out loans for prestigious cars, for instance!

Managers of other companies have occasionally said to me that the staff must be queuing round the block when we tell them that there is a pot of money in the bank and that they only have to ask for it. The usual reaction from other companies is to laugh and say, 'If we did that there wouldn't be any money left after half an hour!' But our staff have never abused the Helping Hand fund.

I often have to force help on people when I find out they have a problem. I am proud that we have built up this culture of decency. You know you've got the culture right if your workers do not try to rip you off.

As well as the subsidised healthcare scheme, anyone who is not satisfied with the service they get from their GP can be referred to my Harley Street doctor at the company's expense. This sounds extravagant, but the cost is usually relatively small for the peace of mind it buys them. It also sends a clear message to staff that this company really takes care of them.

Promoting from within

A key part of our loyalty to staff is our principle of only promoting from inside the company.

I am often told that organisations need fresh blood, but I find the only time you need to bring in fresh people at senior level is if you require specialist skills. The only senior post we have needed to fill from outside was that of finance director.

Clearly, if you are building a company from scratch or trying to turn round an organisation that has been poorly managed, you will need to bring in your own team of people that you can rely on, but I am sceptical when I hear people claim that their company would do so much better if only they could replace their managers or had a greenfield site as far as their workforce is concerned.

Most organisations could do a lot better with the managers they already have if they did more to motivate them.

We take the view that if you are the best in your field, you don't need fresh blood at senior level because you already have the quality people you need inside the organisation.

There are many sound reasons for keeping promotion internal. We know our people very well and can make good judgements about whether they would be suitable for the job on offer. I believe that however skilled you are at interviewing, you can't really know a new person until they have been with the company for a while.

It is also very demotivating for everyone else to bring in outsiders above the heads of existing staff. People become disillusioned and resentful when they see promotion opportunities closed off. In many organisations, schemes that bring in graduates at senior levels have created nothing but trouble, with inexperienced managers and a hostile workforce.

I have nothing against accelerated development, but we fast-track people only according to ability and performance, and not according to qualifications, colour, age, sex, length of service or what school they went to. We employ graduates, but they start at the bottom like everyone else. Very often they do achieve rapid promotion, but only because they show real ability. Graduates who are willing to work their way up have gained the respect of their colleagues.

A company that is growing slowly and steadily should always have good people coming up through the ranks. To fit the right people into the right jobs you have to be able to try them out, which means you must be quick to promote but also quick to demote. We are always ready to allow people to have a go at a job, but if they can't handle it they go straight back to their old job with no fuss. We do not believe in promoting people to their level of incompetence.

In a relatively small company like ours, it can be difficult to find new challenges for people who deserve promotion. At Richer Sounds we have found a way of keeping up the momentum of promoting from within by developing dual roles. Many of our people, from senior managers to sales assistants, have a second job within the organisation (see Chapter 5). As well as adding variety to their role and stretching their abilities, it ensures that the company makes the most of their experience and skills.

What happens when people want to leave? We do our best to hang on to good staff, but as ours tend to be young and adventurous, we acknowledge that some might suddenly get the bug to go and work in the US for a year, say, or travel round the world.

So, provided that people talk to us first about their plans, we don't give them a hard time. Gaining outside experience can be useful to people in their career and, at the very least, it stops people feeling frustrated in the shop because they are really hankering after white-water rafting in Australia.

Wherever possible, we try to fit people back in if they want to re-join us when they get home. It is not usually possible to give cast-iron guarantees beforehand, because no one knows what the vacancy situation will be in a year or two's time, but in many cases we have been able to accommodate them on their return. We do not want our good people to feel trapped.

The important thing is for people to talk to us about what they want. If people tell us, we can nearly always help them, but we're not sympathetic if a member of staff packs it in without warning and then turns up a year later wanting their old job back. All my staff have met me and know they can discuss things with me or the directors, so there is no excuse for people not to talk it over first before they take a big step like leaving the company.

No one enjoys their job every day of their lives, but my advice to people is always that, before they run off in hope of finding a 'better' job, they should draw up a balance sheet, setting out the pros and cons of their work now. There is no such thing as the perfect job and Richer Sounds does not pretend to be that, but, overall, I believe we offer a better package than most in our industry, so a balance sheet could help people look more objectively at what they've got. They might find they've become preoccupied with one or two problems and have overlooked all the good things. It would be a mistake to walk out on a job because of some negative aspects – which might be easily dealt with – only to regret it later. This applies as much to senior managers as it does to more junior staff. The trick is to build in safety valves to prevent this happening (more on this later).

Loyalty for us is not a vague principle but a direct personal relationship between senior management (including myself) and each member of staff. From day one, we give them our phone numbers and tell them to ring us if they have a problem, either work or personal. We make a point of being accessible and we find that they really appreciate that.

So there are my five ways to motivate people. I'm sure most good employers will recognise their value.

Motivation comes from a combination of these factors and people will respond differently to different schemes. Some are turned on by competitions; others don't need the competitive element, but thrive in the knowledge that they are appreciated. So ideally you need a web of initiatives covering your organisation.

Measure your motivation

How do you know if people are well motivated? This is where organisations seem to be amazingly primitive. Their skills in measuring motivation are terribly underdeveloped, and many employers have never thought to measure motivation levels at all.

So here are a few good methods of measuring motivation.

Labour turnover

If people are leaving your organisation at a rapid rate, it is very likely that they're not happy! This is the crudest yardstick to measure motivation.

Obviously, you not only need to measure the turnover of people who leave voluntarily (although if you are firing a lot of staff because they are not up to the job, perhaps you should look at your recruitment techniques).

We do not count those who leave within a few weeks of joining because they could not take the pace, who decided they didn't like selling or customers (!), or felt they didn't fit in. Staff have to work hard and it is inevitable that some recruits will not be up to it. It is better to find that out early on, so we do not regard it is a failure on our part if they leave.

The ones to measure are the established staff who resign through dissatisfaction. As far as Richer Sounds is concerned, our voluntary labour turnover is practically zero. In twenty-two years we have had only a small handful leave to join the competition.

Over the years, people have left us to do a range of other things, from going to Bible College to working with the handicapped, and we have wished them well. People wanting to broaden their horizons or change careers certainly does not reflect badly on your management. If colleagues leave because they are frustrated or disappointed, it does. Good managers ought to know exactly why people are leaving.

It is best to measure your labour turnover against your industry average, but remember that low turnover is no guarantee that people are happy. They may be staying only because there are no other jobs locally to go to.

Absenteeism

The national average absenteeism rate is 4–5 per cent. In my company the rate is between 1 and 2 per cent.

If you are treating your staff well and they are happy working for you, they will take fewer days off sick. Everyone knows that a proportion of days 'sick' are nothing to do with illness. When people are genuinely ill, stress often plays a large part, which is why we insist on our managers and staff working no more than five days a week and taking their holidays.

The real reasons for absenteeism are often hard to pin down. Clearly, if people say they are sick, you must assume that they are telling the truth and treat the matter sensitively, but if you suspect the sickness is not genuine, one of the most effective ways of tackling it is through peer pressure. Colleagues can be much quicker than managers to identify and comment when someone is swinging the lead.

As a consultant, I advised a retail chain where very many of the shop staff were off sick on a Saturday. Why? It was not because some mysterious bug went round on a Friday night. It was really because their families wanted them home on Saturdays.

We tackled this specific issue by publishing the percentage rate of absenteeism by branch and department. Focusing on individual absentees can be unfair, but tackling the department rate as a whole produced results. It created a lot of peer pressure and worked dramatically well, bringing absenteeism down, with enormous cost savings for the company.

In many cases, branch managers knew who the worst offenders were. These were the kind of people who knew exactly how many days of paid sick leave they were entitled to every year and always managed to take their 'entitlement'. They were taking the mickey and the answer was to embarrass them into changing their ways by showing how they were letting their colleagues down.

Theft

If people are happy and well motivated, they are far less likely to steal. People might start pilfering small amounts because they are bored or large amounts because they are in serious financial trouble. We have systems in place to prevent either situation.

Employees also frequently cheat on their employer if they feel the business is cheating on them. If they have to work long hours without overtime, they start bumping up their expense claims and so on. In some organisations this is ingrained in the culture. So exploiting your staff rarely pays in the long term.

Customer service

I would bet that if you have a branch or department generating a high level of customer complaints, its labour turnover, absenteeism and shrinkage rates would all be high, its profitability low and the staff would be unhappy. These factors are inescapably related.

An attitude survey

The first four items on this list are broad measures, essentially indicators of whether you have a motivation problem or not.

The best way of all to measure motivation is to carry out an attitude survey, asking people directly what they think about their jobs. An example of the Richer Sounds Attitude Survey is given in Appendix A, along with the results.

Ideally, attitude surveys should be carried out no more than once a year. There is no need to have them more frequently than that because staff will get fed up with them, but it is important to undertake them regularly. On the other hand, if you only do one, people will regard it as a worthless exercise.

The point is that it does not matter too much what the first year's results say. What matters is whether there is any difference from the previous figures. The first survey is mainly to give you a benchmark against which to measure the success of your drive for improvement.

Some of the companies I have advised say they are not keen on attitude surveys. I usually find they did one five years ago, did not like what their staff said, blamed the consultants for asking the wrong questions and buried the results in a filing cabinet.

Basic principles to follow are that the survey shouldn't be too long and tedious and the questions should be easy to understand. Our survey asks them how far they agree or disagree with a range of propositions, for example: 'We work very much as a team in my store/department', 'I feel I could do my manager's/head of department's job better than them', 'Customers are number one at Richer Sounds'.

The survey must be anonymous to have credibility. People will not be honest if they think they can be found out. We used to get very good results from our surveys, but we had a suspicion these results were too good to be true. So in 1994 we changed the way we did it. Instead of the surveys being sent to central support office, a sales assistant in Birmingham was put in charge of compiling the results. All envelopes were addressed to him and he destroyed the returns afterwards, so it was made clear to everybody that senior management could not see who said what.

The results from that survey were slightly worse than in previous years and we think that was due to the change in the system. Now it is carried out via an online form and, if colleagues wish, it can still be completed anonymously.

People must also be encouraged to fill in the survey. They won't feel like doing it when they get home at the end of the day. It is better for the branch or department to set aside half an hour in company time for everyone to do it. This will produce a larger response rate and the more people who participate in the survey, the more meaningful it is.

We are then committed to responding to the issues raised and a summary of the feedback is published for all colleagues to see. I am pleased to say that in 2016, 94 per cent agreed that customers were number one. Other responses gave us more pause for thought, for example, 15 per cent felt procedures took preference over serving customers well, so customer service was their top priority for improvement.

Apart from being a good barometer of staff motivation, an attitude survey is also full of useful material for managers.

The way to analyse the results is to weigh the scores according to the importance of the questions. The scores can then be added up and compared year on year for the same questions.

Accounting for motivation

Using these measures, it is not difficult to draw up the balance sheet of motivation. Labour turnover, absenteeism, theft and poor customer service are all direct costs to your organisation.

Labour turnover

It typically costs £5,000 to recruit and train a new staff member. So in an organisation of 1,000 staff, 20 per cent staff turnover is costing one million pounds a year. Reducing turnover to 10 per cent saves £500,000.

Absenteeism

When people are off sick, you are paying them not to work. So in that organisation employing 1,000 and paying, say £50 a shift, a 4 per cent absenteeism rate is costing £2,000 a day. Again, halving the absenteeism rate brings enormous savings, not to mention improving customer service and lifting the pressure on the rest of the staff.

Theft

Theft is a direct loss to any organisation. In the retail industry shrinkage is typically 1–2 per cent. At Richer Sounds our stocktakes confirm we have barely 0.1 per cent. The difference for us is well over £2 million a year.

Customer complaints

The textbooks say that every unhappy customer will tell up to twenty other people about the poor service they received, but only one customer in twenty bothers to complain directly to the service provider.

This means that for every complaint you receive, there could be nineteen other dissatisfied customers complaining to their friends – which means that up to 400 potential customers have heard bad things about you. So if you are selling £10 products, you may have lost £4,000 worth of business for every complaint you receive.

The thing to remember about complaints is that, paradoxically, it is best to invite as many of them as possible. If you receive no complaints, this does not necessarily mean that customers are happy. It could mean that they have not bothered, or are unable, to come back to you.

At Richer Sounds, we would rather people complained to us than to their friends. If they tell us the problem, we can put it right and we hope to turn an unhappy customer into a happy one. So our aim is to make it easy for people to complain, to get that one-in-twenty ratio down. If one in five dissatisfied customers complains directly to you, that figure of lost business per complaint goes down to £800.

Keep the buzz

My point about motivation is that it does not have to be left to chance. It does not depend on whether your work is exciting and glamorous, or whether you are lucky enough to have a model workforce and charismatic managers. Nor is it only small companies that can motivate their people: every organisation can introduce systems for motivating its employees better.

What managers often forget is that you have to keep coming up with new ideas. What seems like a wonderful perk one year will be taken for granted the next. It is only human nature to want more. In their personal lives people are always looking for something extra. Every year they want to add something to their house, or get a better car, or have a more exciting holiday. These are normal aspirations and it is no different at work. After all, if people did not have aspirations for something new and better, companies like mine would not stay in business.

Management's job is to keep the excitement going and this is the hardest part of motivation. Every year I think about what we can do next year. There needs to be a drip-feed of new incentives and benefits. If you give people all the goodies all at once, they will soon take them for granted. It is better to bring them in at intervals, with every year the prospect of something exciting ahead.

So never forget about motivation. Keep up with the incentives and rewards, the thank-you letters, the communication, and continually improve the way you treat your employees. It is hard work, but the benefits are enormous. Once you start measuring the payback on your investment in the workforce, you will see real financial results, as well as hopefully sleeping better at night!

5

Recruiting the right people, and keeping them

In any organisation that deals with the public, its reputation is on the line every time one of its employees serves a customer, or even just speaks to them on the phone. So it is astonishing how little attention some companies pay to the selection and training of their front-line staff.

Maybe this is not so surprising, considering that dealing with customers is deemed to be the lowest grade job in most companies and public services in Britain – which only goes to show what those organisations must think about their customers.

We have turned this on its head at Richer Sounds and treat the interface with the customer as the most important part of the business, so we go to a lot of trouble to recruit the right people and train them well and, once we've got them, we hang on to them. Recruitment and training are costly and we make sure we don't throw that investment away by allowing staff to leave because they are bored and see no future in the job.

The selection of staff is one of the most important decisions it is possible to make in a company. Once someone is working for you, they are responsible for thousands of decisions in your name. They are your ambassadors: no matter how junior they are, as far as the customer they are serving is concerned, they represent the company.

How do you find good staff?

The first question you should ask is: who is the right kind of person for my organisation? Some employers have totally unrealistic ideas. You do not need to be a Harvard MBA graduate to operate a till.

Since we are a retailer, you might expect Richer Sounds to be seeking red-hot salespeople. Not at all. The most important quality we look for is friendliness. If people have inherent friendliness, enthusiasm and common sense, they will make good members of the team. Everything else they need can be taught, but you cannot train someone to be genuinely friendly. If they have enthusiasm they will want to learn and if they've got common sense they are able to learn.

Because we regard selling as incidental to customer service, we look for an open, pleasant personality above all. The selling follows from having the right people and the right procedures. I don't think we have ever had an employee who was nice and friendly but couldn't sell.

Recruitment

Taking on a new member of staff is one of the most difficult decisions a manager makes, but there are ways of minimising the risks.

For a start, it obviously helps if you attract people who like what you do. If we put an ad in the newspaper we get people who ask 'Richer who?', but when we advertise for staff in our own catalogue we get applications from people who know exactly what we do. They are already fans and they are ready to consider working for us.

As the ad in our catalogue says, 'Some of our best staff were customers.' That way, we attract people who already love our products and know what goes on in our shops. They have seen how hard we work. The downside is that because 95 per cent of our customers are male we nearly always only attract applications from men through the catalogue. We are keen to increase the proportion of women in the company, so we also advertise more widely.

We have an introduce-a-friend scheme that has been very successful. Employees who introduce someone into the company get a £100 bonus after their friend has been with us six months. This scheme is based on the premise that friends are likely to know what we do because they have heard their mates talk about their job in the pub. If they've also seen our chaps tumble out of the shop exhausted after a hard day and they still want to work for us, they've got the right attitude.

The other advantage is that if it's a friend, we will know something about their background and character, and our employees usually introduce like-minded people they think will fit in.

So we rarely need to advertise in the mainstream papers, especially as we have very little staff turnover. People respond to our catalogue adverts all the time and everyone who writes in is given an initial telephone interview. You can't tell everything about a person on the phone, but you can at least tell how friendly and pleasant they sound, and it weeds out those who can't handle a phone call.

Between 25 and 50 per cent of applicants do well on the phone and, if so, we tell them to visit their local Richer Sounds shop manager for an interview. They can then be shortlisted for future vacancies. So when we open a new branch, we have a ready-made pool of applicants in the nearby area that we can select from.

Trial run

When vacancies arise, we always try people first. People usually either over-perform or under-perform in an interview. Some people seem impressive in interviews, but it's all talk and after a week in the job they start coming in late for work.

The only way to tell how good someone will really be is to get them stuck in to the job. We give applicants a trial day, or a week, or two weeks, until we are happy that they can make the grade.

Trial periods are vital, because taking on people who drop out after a few weeks is a costly waste of time for all involved. We need to know if people can take the pressure. They may think we are a nice company selling wonderful hi-fis and TVs, but can they put up with cleaning out the stockroom?

Once they pass the trial period, they get taken onto the payroll, but first, every single new shop recruit has to be seen and approved by me or the operations director. I like to see them first to be sure that they are nice people. You can only know this by meeting someone face-to-face. It's very hard to change someone who has a personality problem, however technically competent they are. I'd much rather have a friendly person who is keen to learn and can be trained.

Meeting new people also shows them that I take an interest in them. I want them to feel loyal to me and meeting them early on sends a message that everyone in this organisation counts.

That is why I always make a point of going to our Virgin Seminar to see the new recruits undergoing their first training. I do at least an hour's talk so that we can see each other.

Support for new staff

So you have a new person on the payroll. The next stage is where many companies fall down. They don't give enough support and training in those crucial first weeks.

At Richer Sounds we give new recruits three things: our welcome pack, a shadow and our Virgin Seminar.

They start their training even before they officially join the company, because we do not let anyone out on the shop floor unprepared. On the first day of their trial they have to read the training manual in the stockroom before they are allowed near the customers.

Once on the payroll, they receive their welcome pack. This is pretty comprehensive, maybe too comprehensive, but I would rather people had too much information than not enough.

Everyone remembers their first day at school and the first day in a new job can have just as much impact. You must introduce the new person to the culture of the organisation right from the start, when they are at their most receptive and eager to learn. It's very important that from day one everyone who joins us is singing from the same hymn sheet.

They must know from the outset what kind of company they're joining. Companies have different missions: some want to go for market share, some for profit. We want to give great value and customer service, and we believe the profit follows. So we set out our mission statement, *The Richer Way*, and show them our organisation chart with the customer at the top. This explains to our recruits, in simple language, what direction the company is trying to go in.

The welcome pack is virtually a small suitcase of information. As well as the *Colleague Handbook* and contract of employment, there is the *What Can We do?* suggestion book, our health and safety policy, health tips and our charter against any type of harassment, plus the telephone numbers of all the branches and directors (with senior directors' home phone numbers, including my own).

There is the *Benefits and Incentives* booklet too, setting out all the things we do for employees, which never fail to impress. We also give them

Living Legends and Disasters – a few examples of superb service or major mistakes in the company – and they can take some lessons from that!

Each recruit also receives an induction DVD, in which I go through the most important points and they get to see what the senior directors look like.

The welcome pack is very important. In most businesses, if you ask who is in charge of training, you're told 'the manager', but let's face it, managers don't have time to train recruits. They have rarely been given any training in how to train and they are always short-staffed, so in practice the training just doesn't happen.

The welcome pack starts the training off, with plenty of information to read and absorb.

My shadow and me

We give everyone a shadow. This is a colleague, a non-manager, whose job it is to put their arm around the new recruit and tell them everything about the business.

The shadow makes sure they have their welcome pack, a uniform and their payroll number. He or she also takes the recruit to the pub (expenses paid) and tells them about this weird long-haired guy who owns the company and what it's all about.

This mother-hen role is important not just for the new recruit but for the shadow, too. They are usually junior staff members, who might have only been with the company themselves for six months, but they are responsible for getting this new person's career off to a good start. Officially, the shadow relationship is for a month; unofficially it often lasts as long as the recruit and his shadow stay with the company.

The shadow takes the recruit through four weeks of tests on the training manual and on basic company procedures.

The sausage machine

Finally, the recruit is sent on a Richer Virgin Seminar. This is an intensive three-day training programme, affectionately known as 'the sausage machine'. Small groups are coached and tested thoroughly on our procedures. They are taken through the training manual more or less line by line, and questioned to see if they have fully understood it.

Very little of this training is about selling. As you might guess, most of it is about customer service. Recruits who have been in sales jobs before say it is completely different to anything they've experienced. They're amazed that the only thing we say about selling is that if customers aren't sure about a purchase, don't push them into it. Then we spend three days telling them how to make customers feel good.

Training is a four-part process. My analysis of training is based on the needs of the retail business, but much of this will also apply to any organisation that has customers in any shape or form.

The first aspect is product or technical training. If you're selling washing machines you need to know what the models are, what the machines do, what the buttons are for, and so on.

The trainee also needs to know about procedures. They must be taught how to write a credit agreement. If you're working in a factory you need to know what to do when, what safety precautions to take, and so on. Every kind of shop, office or industry will have its own procedures and normally this is the one thing that people get trained in (more or less well).

Thirdly, in a commercial environment you need to know how to sell. Many companies spend a lot of time on this but we tend to downplay the selling. We don't teach people how to push a customer to close the sale – in fact, just the opposite – but of course there are useful sales techniques that can be taught and we focus on these in our training, for instance, how to sell appropriate accessories profitably and in an ethical way. This is a considerable challenge and one that we work very hard on – there's a massive amount they need to learn if they are to understand the benefits and features of all the comparable products we carry in our stores so they can sell honestly.

How often has a sales assistant tried to persuade you to part with more cash by running down the product you've asked for? 'Oh no, you don't want to buy one of those, you'll find it won't last more than six months.' This is not good for the shop as it suggests the company is selling poor quality goods. A much more positive way is to explain what the customer could get for, say, £50 more and let them make up their own mind.

The fourth part of training is in customer service: how to approach the customer, how to help them, the right things to say, how to really work hard at making customers happy.

I find that organisations are generally not good at technical or product training and poor at customer service training. I have come across companies that boast about their training, but that do no customer service training at all, apart from 'closing the sale' (often using ways that offer the customer no service at all).

The sausage machine is intensive and demanding, and we won't apologise for that. We want the best people who can stand up to high pressure, because working in one of our shops three days before Christmas is very demanding. We tell trainees that if the job was easy, everyone would be as good as us.

The regime is tough, but we find that people rise to the challenge and are proud of completing the course. There is a very low dropout rate from the training.

I sometimes ask the shop manager after a new staff member returns from this seminar to find out how they have got on. The answer I always hear is that they have come back a different person. Once they have been on this training, they are like a coiled spring, ready to give real customer service and try out everything they've learnt.

New recruits have to wear a trainee's name badge until they have been on their Virgin Seminar. They also have to give us confidence that they are capable of giving our customers a positive service experience before they can take off this badge.

Some protest and say it's embarrassing, but I tell them they have to wear their L-plates. If you're driving behind a car with L-plates on that keeps stalling, you don't start hooting – you give the learner driver a chance. In the same way, customers are easier on trainees.

If a trainee doesn't wear a badge and they don't know the answers to customers' questions, it looks as if we employ idiots. So it's a protection device for both the staff and the company.

Continuous development

Training is all too often completely overlooked by many employers. You can find people who have been with a company twenty years but who have received no training since their initial induction course. Yet organisations change every day and you therefore need to update all your staff on a regular basis.

At Richer Sounds, training carries on all the way through people's careers, with regular seminars for managers and deputy managers, and ongoing training for all the sales colleagues. We tend not to call it training and perhaps colleagues don't always notice that they are being trained, but the seminars provide a lot for them to learn, as well as being opportunities for communication and team building.

Some people are surprised to discover that we don't open our doors until midday Monday to Friday, but we use the mornings to train our colleagues on a daily basis, with sessions on technology, customer service, selling and, the biggest by far, product knowledge. We can only hope to sell ethically if we know our products inside and out, which is what we aim to do. (The only downside to this is that we can't recruit extra staff at busy periods because they wouldn't know what they were doing.)

We have also developed technical training schemes to teach employees more about the products we sell. You don't need to be a complete hi-fi buff to work for us, but the more you know, the better the service you can offer to customers. So we now have technical courses leading to bronze, silver and gold awards.

This is continuous development. Training is not about putting people through a course and forgetting about them. Many companies will send staff on hugely expensive courses, but give them no opportunities for further development. All the new ideas for the business that are stimulated by the training are not allowed to lead anywhere. There is a cut-off and people are just left to muddle along.

In my company, everyone is being continuously developed, just as the business is being continuously improved. If there are new initiatives, everyone has to learn about them. The seminars are one way of bringing people up to date, but there are other methods we use all the time, such as the weekly tapes. Staff want to know about the new things that are happening – so talk to them.

Interviewing – the more the merrier

If your company attracts a lot of applicants for posts, or if you have to recruit large numbers, perhaps for the opening of a new branch, I recommend group interviews.

Ideally you will have some sort of application form to screen people initially, at least to rule out those who are totally unsuitable.

Don't place too much emphasis on CVs. Employers tend to think it is important to see whether an applicant has experience, but how much does this really matter? When we are born we have no experience of anything, but that doesn't mean we are written off as human beings – we hopefully have potential.

In my company we recruit people all the time for jobs that on paper they are completely unqualified for, but we can tell from the interview that they will fit in and do well. My chosen successor started as a junior buyer and is now the IT director.

So there is no substitute for seeing people face-to-face. It is much more cost effective to get ten or twenty people in at a time than singly for interviews. If you see them in as a group, you can afford to spend much more time with them. Rather than fifteen minutes each with twenty people, you can spend two hours and get to know them much better.

They will also know you better and you will have the time to explain fully and demonstrate, if possible, exactly what the job entails.

Give the applicants badges to wear and watch them closely. After a couple of hours you can gain a very good idea of who looks right, who is smiling and enthusiastic, who asks the right questions and answers well. People will show their true colours much more than in a traditional interview, where they are intimidated under the spotlight.

Group interviews can work for almost any sort of job. We held one to fill a post for an accountant and twenty-six applicants attended. We did a talk for them all and then split them into small groups to get to know them better. Although the overall calibre was high, we managed to spot the person who was right for the job.

Once you've narrowed down the field from twenty to six, you will want to interview them individually. Psychometric tests are trendy now, but I have my doubts about whether you can really get to know people from a test. At best, you can see very crudely if someone is a team player or not. A test can't tell you if they are honest or polite, or if they will get out of bed on time for work.

It's important to do the character tests before you make people fill out written applications. Sometimes firms go through lengthy administrative checks on applicants before they look at their character. That's the wrong way round: find out first if they are the kind of people who will fit into your organisation.

At Richer Sounds, we take a lot of trouble to follow up references. Because integrity is so important to us, we ask some very searching questions to see if people have any previous criminal convictions. We even ask them to obtain a copy of their record from the police computer, which they are entitled to do under the Data Protection Act. This may seem extreme, but our shops handle large amounts of cash so it is vital that people are honest.

Before we brought in these safeguards we discovered two managers who were cheating us, both of whom had falsely denied having any previous convictions.

We will not automatically reject someone who has a previous conviction: it depends what they did and whether they have changed their ways since then. The more important point in our eyes is that they tell us the truth.

Assessments – good and bad

Once an employee has been with the company six months, we give them a career counselling session to see how they are getting on.

This is very different from the annual assessments that most organisations carry out. I regard annual assessments as the worst possible way to deal with your staff. What's wrong with annual assessments? For a start, any well-run company should know how its staff is doing at any moment in time. It shouldn't have to stop and take a look once a year. It should be measuring their performance continually.

If you have to sit down with your staff to find out how they're doing, as a manager you're not doing your job properly. You should already be familiar with the quality of their work.

An annual assessment is purely a snapshot, it captures the employee's performance at that time, their views and moods (and the manager's) on that day only. People aren't machines: they have their ups and downs and so a snapshot is not a realistic portrayal of anyone's performance. Too often the assessment is carried out in a rush to hit some arbitrary deadline.

Assessments can be very intimidating, especially as they are normally linked to pay rises. Just as some people do badly in interviews, some otherwise good people get freaked out over assessments and do not do themselves justice.

Who benefits from assessments anyway? Given that the manager should already know how well the employee is doing, an assessment should be for the benefit of the employee. It should be a chance for them to talk about their career. That is very important, but, as I said, people aren't machines. On the day of the assessment, things might be going well. Two days later, they might have an argument with their supervisor, or decide they want to do something different. Do they have to wait 363 days for their next assessment before they can raise these issues?

Career counselling

We don't have annual assessments at all at Richer Sounds. We see people after six months to have a chat, find out how happy they are and see what direction they want to go in. What happens from then on is that all members of staff can, at any time, have career counselling.

Career counselling takes a high priority with us and is enshrined in the company's philosophy. It means that, whenever they like, an employee can request a meeting with a senior person in order to discuss their career, whether there is a specific problem or whether they are concerned with their whole future direction.

This is an important safety valve. We don't want people telling us they weren't happy at work after they've handed in their notice. They must have the opportunity to talk to someone whenever they want.

A lot of employers will say that of course their staff can talk to their managers at any time, but that's just the problem. Managers know the staff best, but nine times out of ten the reason staff are not happy is because of that very manager!

The danger of seeing someone more senior, say the area manager, is that they might not know that staff member very well. Internal politics also come into play. Career counselling sessions are often requested because people are interested in moving to other parts of the business. If you tell the area manager, they get annoyed by you wanting to move to the marketing department and advise you against it.

So we have taken the radical step of allowing the employees to choose who they go to for career counselling. It can be anyone – including me. I have done a number of career counselling sessions, including ones with quite junior staff. The fact that I am willing to do this sends a powerful message to both staff and senior managers – the boss has time for you. If I can spare the time for career counselling, senior managers can too. It is never easy to find the time, but a half-hour chat could be the most effective thirty minutes you have ever spent if it persuades a staff member with ten years' experience not to leave the company.

New challenges

We don't want people to stagnate in our company. We want them to be continuously developing and full of fresh ideas, but we're not a huge company and over the years we've grown quite slowly, so there are not unlimited promotion prospects for everyone. Nevertheless, we've found ways to keep people stimulated and stretched.

As I mentioned earlier, our principle is: quick to promote, quick to demote. We give people a go. Management cannot always know exactly if someone is suitable for a certain job, so the best thing is to try them out. This works as long as you create a climate in which people are allowed to fail.

In most organisations, managers are scared to demote people, so, as I argued earlier, staff are simply promoted to their level of incompetence.

At Richer Sounds, we accept that people are allowed a shot at a job, but they won't always succeed. If someone is demoted, it may be uncomfortable for a week or so, but there is no lasting stigma. It might be thought that once someone is demoted, they will lose enthusiasm and their work will go downhill, but that is not our experience. In fact, it is surprising how many times I've demoted people and they've thanked me afterwards. They said they had been out of their depth, or unhappy, and were glad to be free of the hassle. People usually know if they're not up to a job, but their pride might stop them from admitting they can't handle it.

Dual roles

As I mentioned in the previous chapter, many people at Richer Sounds have another role for the company as well as their main job. Four are store inspectors visiting the stores, two of our store managers help our operations team with the recruitment and training of our colleagues and several other store managers are part of the buying team. Others help with the property side of things, write questions for the training tests, are involved with merchandising or help to produce our staff magazine.

This sounds as if we have found a clever way of saving money by making people work harder, and it does mean huge cost savings to the business, but that is not the only reason why we do it. We do it to make people's jobs more interesting and to knit the company together. We find that in practice the primary jobs do not suffer, people are challenged and more fulfilled, and they get to know the business better. After all, what's the point of having a training manager with no hands-on experience of the job?

We have members of staff who will not get any higher in the company, but I do not want them to get bored and frustrated. Nor do I want people with potential to leave us because they see no prospects. As soon as anyone is doing well, accomplishing their existing role easily and flexing their muscles a bit, we look for something else for them to do. Believe me, we're very good at finding things for people to do because everyone is generating new ideas.

A successful shop manager might be made a shop inspector responsible for overseeing stores' merchandise and procedures, for example.

This is a much better system than having area managers overseeing the branches. I don't believe in having full-time area managers, because once they no longer have their own shop, they are not leading from the front and they lose respect. They are also expensive! Looking at area managers in other firms, I've never yet seen one who had a real routine that I was happy with. The danger is that they end up swanning around in company cars, filling in for staff who are off sick.

Doing two jobs can really bring out the best in people. For the colleagues doing this, their own shops must always come first and that shop's performance must never be allowed to slip, but this has rarely been a problem. The second role improves their job variety, gives them a little more reward and a lot more status.

It also allows people to get out of the confines of their department or branch and get involved in decision-making for the company as a whole. They meet colleagues from other parts of the country and know they are contributing at a national level.

Staff are encouraged to put themselves forward for new roles. We also rely on them to tell us if they want to change jobs, apply for a promotion or move to a different part of the country. If people want to be managers we say, 'Put yourself on the shortlist.'

Sometimes a member of staff might swap with a counterpart in another branch. It is a way of adding variety to the job and picking up new ideas. We also encourage people to do other things: for example, if anyone wants to get involved with our charity foundation or join the Colleagues' Council, we will pay for a reasonable amount of their time.

In the firing line?

There might still remain the problem people – the ones who are just not doing a good job. We usually find people who don't fit into the company or can't take the pressure soon drop out of their own accord, but what about the ones who do not seem to have what it takes?

We don't give up on people easily. We had a sales assistant join us at a very busy store. After a while it became clear he was struggling and his own manager didn't have the time or the patience to work with him, but the manager at another shop offered to take him on. That sales assistant has been with us for several years now, has been promoted to assistant manager and is a valued member of the team. I was delighted that we could develop him and there are many other examples of people who have been moulded into shape by a good manager.

To really know whether staff are good enough, you need sensitive managers who are measuring the performance of their staff well, watching them and observing them. Sometimes people limp along in a new job for quite a while and then suddenly get the hang of it. So you have to balance that with the 'quick to promote, quick to demote' principle.

On the whole, it's much cheaper (as well as ethically better) to keep the people you've got, in whom you have invested time and money, than to get rid of them and find someone new. It comes back, as I said at the start, to whether they have that basic friendliness and common sense.

Redeployment can work very well if you don't pigeonhole people and assume they are only suitable for a certain type of job. When we found we were overstaffed in the warehouse, we offered jobs elsewhere, with retraining, and now have three ex-warehouse staff working in the accounts department.

We rarely fire anyone, except for dishonesty. We've never fired anyone because they couldn't sell. It's highly unlikely we would get rid of anyone for making a mistake either, as long as they admitted it and learnt from it. If they carry on doing a bad job, arriving late for work, continually making mistakes, and so on, we get together.

We do like to hire for attitude and train for skill, as we prefer by a factor of 100 per cent to have a friendly colleague we can teach, than a grumpy know-all!

Punctuality is one of the things we measure and any cumulative lateness is reported directly to me. Because we have good measures, staff know if they are heading for the edge and they have no excuse for not doing something about it. All the rules of employment are set out in the welcome pack, in a friendly way, but so that there is no ambiguity.

Dishonesty is the really unacceptable crime. I once found a manager and staff smoking marijuana in one shop after hours. I might not have considered this automatically a sacking offence, but for the fact that they brazenly denied doing anything – despite clouds of smoke filling up the shop! I fired them because they had lied to me.

We are merciless against anyone found defrauding us and we make it clear to everyone that honesty is paramount. We warn staff they cannot sit on the fence – they are either preventing fraud or assisting it. If they know a colleague is stealing and do not tell us, they are colluding and will be dismissed when we find out.

We also reward people if they tell us of any suspicion of theft. For any information that results in a prosecution, they receive £1,000. Where it is not possible to prosecute, we will still make some sort of reward. In fact, nearly all of our discoveries of fraud have arisen from reports by local members of staff.

Only human

It might be nice to have a workforce of super-intelligent people, all obedient and cheerful, willing to work ten hours a day and never take a day off sick, but so far I haven't managed to find these paragons. We settle for nice, friendly people, who make mistakes and have their days off but are basically willing and enthusiastic.

I suppose we have really two types of people working for us. We have exceptional people and we have ordinary people who are exceptionally dedicated. As a rule, if I had to choose I would probably prefer the latter. They tend to be more loyal, less spoilt and less likely to 'grass hop' between jobs.

We then train them up, get them involved in the business, look after them and motivate them. We get great loyalty from all our staff because we are committed to them and look for commitment in return.

The trend these days is away from commitment, to part-time working and short-term or, even worse, zero-hour contracts. Part-time working can be convenient for both the employers and the employee, but it is not convenient for the customer if the part-timers are under-trained and uncommitted. Customers want well-informed staff who won't push them into hasty decisions and will be there again two weeks later if they come back with a problem.

We make sure our part-timers have the same commitment to a career with us as full-timers, even though they are working fewer hours. Where possible, we like part-timers we can develop in to full-timers who will receive the same benefits, so they are just as knowledgeable and motivated.

The responsibility for developing a good workforce rests squarely on managers. Good managers must take an interest in their staff, be constantly aware of their performance and know their strengths and weaknesses. A large part of the solution to the difficult challenge of having good staff is putting the right people in the right jobs. A good manager must spot potential and make the most of it. After all, there are very few perfect people around – and if I found any I probably couldn't afford them!

Already I can hear a cry go up from managers throughout the land – 'I'd love to do all that, but I don't have the time!' It's true that too many managers get bogged down in doing things that don't matter, leaving them no time to do the really important things. So – get organised.

6

How managers should manage themselves

Having read this far, you might be thinking, 'I already work hard and do all the things he's suggesting to manage and motivate my staff. I'll have to put in twenty-five hours a day!'

Well, relax. I don't work twenty-five hours a day and I have no intention of ever doing so. I'm definitely not one of these manic businessmen who have never taken a day off in fifteen years. Given the chance, I like to be out in the Yorkshire countryside with my wife, walking the dogs.

People often don't seem to believe this. 'But you do so much,' they say! I am a major shareholder in three different businesses, visit all my branches around the country, actively support many charities, travel quite a bit, manage and play in a busy band and have quite wide-ranging interests: how do I do it?

I don't do anything like as much as people who are running the country or multinational corporations, but I manage to do a fair amount. As well as the business, I like to spend time reading, watching movies and I also have a good social life and lots of time at home.

When I started my business, I worked very hard. I still work hard because I enjoy what I do, but the point is, I'm not a workaholic. I'm actually quite lazy really. What I mean is, I don't like to do more work than is necessary, I like to do things as easily as possible, as simply as possible, and achieve as much as possible in the time allowed. I don't like to waste my time.

I can do this because I'm organised. I've worked extremely hard at trying to develop the art of running a business effectively, with the minimum of effort.

Less work – more success

This has been a deliberate strategy on my part. A few years ago, I asked myself what I wanted out of my career. I realised I wanted to do less work and have more free time, but I also wanted more financial success.

There is nothing very surprising in that. I'm sure most people, given the choice, would like to work less for more pay. They probably think that unfortunately they do not have the choice, but if you look carefully at how you organise yourself, you might be surprised at what you can achieve. However, a lot of people running organisations apparently want to work harder and harder. Or maybe they don't want to, but they feel they ought to or the work just gets out of control.

So the thing to ask yourself is not what do you want out of the business, but what do you want out of life?

I wanted to be more successful, but work less, so I set about organising myself so that I could spend less time in the office. To begin with, this meant I spent only one week in two in the office and had the other week free. I began to use this time to expand my experience by taking on consultancy work. By being organised in this way, I was also able to concentrate on developing other businesses.

I now am only in the office around two mornings a month as technology means that I can work from wherever I am. This would not be possible if I were not well organised. I couldn't focus on that this happens my other interests unless I could be confident that Richer Sounds was running on the right lines, so I have the systems in place to ensure this.

Expanding your activities is a challenge, but it's fun. Just like my colleagues, I don't want to get stuck in a rut. If you can fit everything in, you should do as much as you can.

The fact that my time is precious helped me in my consultancy work.[‡] Professional consultants tend to be greeted with scepticism, because everyone knows that the longer they take to do a job the more they get paid. I was the opposite. I didn't earn my living from consultancy fees, so I had no conflict of interest. I liked to do a good job in as short time as possible.

I also found that people liked a consultant who is an all-round entrepreneur, rather than a specialist. I haven't been to Harvard and I wasn't just giving them the theory out of a textbook: I offered ideas I knew could work in practice.

Anyone who owns a business is actually doing their company a favour by spending less time in the office. The value of that business is greater if it can be shown to run itself. It is no good making yourself the linchpin of the entire company, because when you come to sell, or in our case hand it over to someone else,[§] the business is worthless if it cannot exist without you.

This can be difficult to come to terms with. People like to feel that they are indispensable and if they've built up an organisation, they can't bear to think it doesn't need them any more, but it will be good for

‡ Long since retired.
§ Richer Sounds is to be left in trust for my colleagues on my demise, similar to John Lewis.

you, your staff and the entire business if the company is not resting solely on your shoulders.

I had a lot of worries when I first decided to do one week on and one week off because I thought my staff would resent it, but I was kidding myself. They don't need me there. When I'm in the office I drive them hard, but then I leave them to get on with their jobs and they love it.

Working one week in two forced me to be organised and to delegate. I learnt that when I am in the office, I have to make sure I am concentrating on the things it is essential for me to do. I can't afford to waste time. I also have to be sure everything is set up to run smoothly when I am not there. It is no good having a week working on something else if the phone rings every two minutes with another crisis in the office.

The key is successful delegation. If you're a bit lazy, like me, either you can end up doing not very much with your life or you can get other people to do work for you. I've always been ambitious, so I learnt how to delegate.

For workaholics, it is even more important to know how to delegate. Without delegation, you cannot make your business grow. Any organisation runs on delegation.

I make sure I only do the minimum. Every job I do, I ask myself: must I do this, or could someone else take it on?

There is a fine balance here, because by doing the minimum, you could lose the respect of your managers and staff. If you're in charge, however much you delegate, you must always be seen to be leading from the front.

I hope I have never lost the respect of my staff. For a start, I know I built the company up on my own. It's not as if I got here with the help of Daddy's money or as if I were brought in over everyone's heads to run a business I knew nothing about.

When Richer Sounds had fewer branches, I was able to spend longer in each. As we've grown, I have had to reassess my priorities. This is The Richer Way – seeing staff are happy first, rather than swanning round the shops on 'royal visits' being 'Mr Big'.

Spending time in the stores keeps me in touch with what's happening and also shows everyone that I am there for them. They are working hard and so am I. This gives them credibility when it comes to delegating. I can honestly say I would never ask someone to do a job that I wouldn't do myself, unless of course I didn't have the technical skills.

It is not necessary for me to check up on shops because we have regular inspections, which are extremely thorough, covering hundreds of points. So if I do occasionally drop in on a shop to see the manager I try not to be critical. For my annual visit, the date is confirmed with the manager in advance because I want the whole team to be present and this needs to be planned on the rota.

Getting organised

The point about being organised is to know what you're doing and to know what everyone else is doing (or supposed to be doing).

You can buy expensive time-management systems these days, for your computer or your personal organiser. However, my own time-management system relies on tried and tested technology – a fine-tip pen and two pieces of A4 narrow-lined paper. I recently upgraded my system to new heights of sophistication with the addition of a plastic cover.

Every second Sunday I sit down and draw up a worksheet for the fortnight ahead. It's a combination of a diary and a to-do list. I fill in my short-term diary for the two weeks ahead. There is still a list of all the people I need to see regularly: my nine directors, my PA and so on, with all the topics I need to talk to them about.

I also itemise: things to talk to the branches about, issues to mention on the weekly message, work to do at home, notes for all the heads of department and the long-term pending list. Every time I draw up a worksheet, I transfer the items outstanding from the last sheet on to the new one.

So when I have a meeting or call with one of my directors, I have an individual list for them on a separate sheet. It tells me what we discussed at the last meeting, what they had to do and what they need to report back to me on. I have drawn up further tasks for them from the main worksheet, which will then be added to their list.

All the senior managers have their own sheets, which include their list of all the tasks they have to report to me about. So, at a glance, everyone knows what they have to do.

I like to keep it all on one sheet – I write very small! I am a great believer in writing everything down.

The beauty of this system is its simplicity and flexibility. It isn't prescriptive: the layout varies according to what I'm doing. It is cheap and foolproof. I can carry it anywhere, it doesn't have batteries that can run out and I can't delete it accidently. The only drawback I've found is that it's susceptible to having coffee spilled on it, which is why I now keep it under a plastic cover.

The sheets can also be kept as a historical record, so it is easy to go back and check what you said to someone or what you asked them to do.

My sheets are very detailed, but I believe in attention to detail. It is linked to our *kaizen* principle

– continuous improvement, remember – which leaves nothing to chance. We are innovative and flexible, but we don't make it up as we go along.

Successful delegation needs attention to detail. It's no good issuing vague instructions or assuming people know what to do. You have to be sure everyone knows exactly what is required and can report back with precise information on what has been done.

How to delegate

Many people do not understand delegation. Delegation is not just about issuing orders. To get people to do things you want, you have to train them, motivate them, know their skills and measure them. Everyone is different and the manager's job is to find out what people are good or not good at. When tasks have been delegated, look at what the person has done well or not so well, and use that information to allocate work the next time.

The important part of delegation is following through. If I give someone ten tasks, unless they think I'm going to check up on them afterwards, they may not bother to do them. They must also know exactly what is expected of them. What is their deadline for these tasks? To what standard must they perform them?

Delegation isn't about dishing out a few instructions and sitting back with your feet up. It's hard work. You have to be organised and meticulous about seeing that work is done.

Some people find it very hard to delegate. They will typically be sole traders, to use a retail term. They'll tell you they cannot get good staff or their managers are not reliable, and it may be true that people do not perform well for them, but the underlying reason is that they can't delegate. They are unable to let go of 'their' business.

Delegation does not mean letting go of responsibility; you are not just leaving people to get on with it, you have to know exactly what has been done. However, you have to let go of your pet notion that you are the only person who can do a job properly. I know this from experience.

I used to do all the buying for Richer Sounds myself. I thought this was the key to a successful business and I thought I did it very well. I prided myself on the wheeling and dealing, charming all the suppliers into giving us great deals. I started taking a couple of my senior managers along to buying meetings with me to watch how it was done. Then came the inevitable day when one of my managers got a better deal than me.

I was very put out at first. No one likes to feel their skills are not irreplaceable, but when I thought about it more objectively I realised this was great. I'd found I couldn't walk on water, but I had also found out I could delegate this whole area of work when I'd always thought I would never be able to let go of the buying side.

This was a real turning point for me in running the company. I had to stand back and let the manager take over the buying. By doing that, we freed up the buying function and allowed it to grow. He set up a buying team, which brings together people from different branches and parts of the company. They have generated lots of new ideas and the whole process has gone from strength to strength.

So sometimes you are forced to delegate, but it is a good lesson to learn. One important point is that when I delegate, I make a real point of standing back. You undermine your team if you delegate to them and then carry on interfering.

When I handed over the buying, suppliers would often try to continue talking to me, but to give my buyer credibility I had to insist he alone placed the orders. I told suppliers I'd talk to them if they had a problem and I was happy to meet them socially, but all the orders had to go through him. Eventually, they stopped approaching me because they realised I'd given him the authority and this became one less call on my time.

So when you're paying someone to do a job, don't tread on their toes. Let them do it and account to you for the results. If their pay is linked to their performance they will have plenty of incentive to produce good results, so let them get on with it.

Keep the information flowing

Essential to successful delegation is having correct management information. Once you have delegated work, the most important thing is to keep your eye on the results. Trying to run a business without accurate management information is like flying a helicopter in fog, at night, without instruments.

You must have systems in place for ensuring you get the information you need, regularly and on time. The management information will obviously vary according to the type of organisation, but every business has to have a set of figures showing how it is doing. Management's duty is to work out what is needed and not ask for impossible and irrelevant data.

In my own business, I get sales figures by branch every six minutes (!) and full detailed figures for all shops every Saturday night.

What is the essential information? I put cash flow at the top of the list. Whatever your business, you have got to know what's coming in and what's going out. I insist on seeing once a week the movements of cash, both actual and projected, thirteen weeks ahead, so I always know what our borrowing requirements are or if there is any cash surplus.

In retail, the stock position is very important. If you see your stock levels rising dramatically but sales levels staying the same, you know that in a matter of weeks you won't be able to pay your bills. Many retailers only think of sales, or profit, forgetting how much money is tied up in stock.

Figures are coming in all the time to show me what is going on. We try to keep the weekly financial information on one sheet of paper, so I'm not spending a lot of time poring over figures, but the main point is that data should come in like clockwork. The minute figures do not come in on time, alarm bells start ringing.

Structure your meetings

Get organised in the way you run your day, too. I'm always amazed how badly people handle meetings, or even phone calls.

When you have delegated work and people report back to you, make sure you structure your meeting with them. Go through their regular, on-going work; check on the progress of the jobs that you gave them at the last meeting; give them their new work and, finally, go over any problems that there might be.

It sounds straightforward, but too many managers don't structure their meetings. They end up not only wasting time, but also not keeping a systematic check on the work that is supposed to have been done. They'll call someone in if there is a problem, or people will come to them with a problem, but that only deals with the work in a random fashion. There may be other areas that are not going well, but no one has noticed so you don't find out until too late.

All the people who report to you need a scheduled opportunity to talk to you. Don't leave them unable to get hold of you, thinking they shouldn't bother you unless the problem is really big, or else trying to avoid you so that you don't find out what is going wrong.

Every one of my executives is given jobs to do, knows exactly what is expected of them and knows that if they have a problem they can use their regular diary slot with me to sort it out.

This also means you will not be ringing your managers and staff continuously to give them more jobs and driving them mad. I ring my managers when it's urgent, but otherwise I leave them undisturbed to get on with things, and they like that.

Cut down meetings

Good, structured meetings with your own managers and staff are invaluable, but do you really need to hold so many meetings with outside people? I suggest you use the phone instead.

Many businesses hold meetings that are unnecessary. By the time someone has come to see you, or you have travelled to meet them, you have talked for an hour and probably had lunch too, you have spent half a day on something that could probably have been dealt with in twenty minutes on the phone.

Always ask yourself, 'Can I do this over the phone or by email?'

Where a meeting is necessary, keep it short. I have an egg timer sitting prominently on my desk and, although I don't use it, it acts as a polite reminder that time is money. However, I would recommend stating at the beginning of a meeting that you only have, say, half an hour, so that everyone present knows at the outset how long they have to get through their business.

Face-to-face meetings are overrated, especially when someone is trying to sell you something. It is good to meet with suppliers at the outset, so they know what you look like, and you should be available if there are problems. Other than that, regular monthly meetings are a waste of time.

Why do companies send their reps out to see people whether their clients want it or not? We generally ban reps from visiting the stores. They hang around, getting in the way of our customers, just so they can fill in their time sheet. It can be a complete waste of their company's time and ours.

Skip lunch!

Even the quickest business lunch takes two hours. I like breakfast meetings or early-evening drinks for business network/contact meetings – they're much more efficient, cheaper and better for the waistline.

Using the phone

When you have an important call to make, stand up. Your mind is much clearer and you're more businesslike if you talk standing up. Try it!*

Be as organised with a phone call as you would a meeting. Always have a pen and paper to hand when you phone someone and prepare a list of the points you want to cover.

* For internal meetings we have a high table we stand at. It keeps speeches short, for obvious reasons.

The phone has its limitations, though. Do not take calls in meetings as it ruins the flow and should not be necessary – you should have a secretary or assistant who can deal with things, at least while you are in the meeting. When you are in a meeting, that's what should take priority. If it is not that important, why are you holding it?

Some things are much better dealt with by letter. I never accept phone calls from customers, for example. That may seem odd, as I go on about customer service so much, but talking on the phone is not the best way of sorting out a customer's problem.

Customers will only tell you their side of the story and I will not comment until I've heard my employee's account. Although I always try to give customers the benefit of the doubt, it is only natural justice and loyalty to my colleagues to hear what they have to say before making a decision.

If I took phone calls from customers, they would think me rude to listen to their complaint and then refuse to commit myself to some action. There's nothing worse than agreeing to make amends and then ringing the shop manager only to find out the customer's story is a complete fiction.

I ask customers to put everything in writing. This gives me their claims, which I can then follow up with the branch. People usually feel better when they've written the letter and got it off their chest.

They also tend to be calmer and politer on paper than on the phone. They have the added acknowledgement of a reply from me.

The working environment

If you are trying to get organised and keep a cool head, make sure the office environment isn't creating problems.

It's great to have a busy office, but you don't want a frantic one, and a competitive atmosphere risks creating a macho culture. I like the idea of open-plan offices, but they can get noisy and disorganised. The macho culture grows because everyone thinks they can see what everyone else is doing and how long they spend at their desks.

Noise can be a real problem and obstacle to working. We put glass partitions into our support offices so people can see each other, but still have some peace and quiet to work.

I find the best thinking time is in the morning; the hours between seven and nine can be the most productive of the day. Do not be frightened to work at home and make good use of those two hours.

You need to forget the macho culture and work out how best to organise your own time. You will be much more effective if you decide how to structure your own day, so that you are making decisions when your mind is clearest. Maybe not everyone is an early bird, but on the whole I think Rockefeller was right when he said that you should never make an important decision after six in the evening. Evenings are for being creative rather than strategic.

Layers of 10

Books, seminars and training courses about management are an incredible growth industry these days, although I'm not sure what they are teaching because nobody seems to be doing the motivating that I think is the really essential job for managers.

Managers are having a hard time now. Everyone from the NHS downwards is 'delayering' – stripping out whole layers of management that are considered redundant. Well, I do not think good management is redundant.

I agree it's a waste of time and money to have too many layers of management in an organisation, but have employers thought sensibly about how many layers they actually need? I have this 'layers of 10' principle: managers cannot manage more than ten people effectively.

This principle is based on my own experience, but it applies in any business I have ever observed.

When I say ten people, it might be twelve at a stretch, but one manager certainly cannot manage thirty people effectively.

The key word here is 'effectively'. To manage people effectively you need to have regular meetings, to delegate jobs to them, to follow through and to see how they are getting on. You also need to be motivating them, coaching them and developing them, as well, of course, as doing your own tasks.

This is a time-consuming job and you cannot do it with more than a dozen people. No one can spend their time managing thirty people in this way.

I have seen managers in charge of maybe twenty-five people; but are they really in charge of them? They're not aware of what half those people are doing at any one time and their staff are not getting access to them. In my view they are not really managing. Managing people means relating to them and working with them individually and directly.

Ten people per manager does not sound very much, but those ten manage ten more people each. With five levels you are managing 100,000 people. If you start taking out layers of management, the organisation cannot work properly. Staff will be under-managed and demotivated.

The board – keep it small

While you need a strong management structure, you don't need a huge board to run a business. Richer Sounds has nine board members, plus my PA.

Businesses should try to avoid big committees. It is hard enough making decisions anyway and the more people you have round the table, the harder it gets. I find that ten people in a meeting is about the maximum practicable if everyone is to participate effectively.

Try to get a good balance of people on the board. Too often, chairs and directors just pick other people like themselves, but you want different points of view and different skills. Of course, what everyone around the table should have in common is business acumen.

Incidentally, it is vital for your business that you train a successor. You should be grooming someone to do your job. A lot of employers are reluctant to do that, especially if they own the company. They think they're going to put themselves out of a job, but apart from making the business more saleable, they have a responsibility to ensure that the company does not fall apart if they fall under a bus one day.

The leadership role

So once I've delegated as much as I can and spend just a fraction of my time in the office, what does my job entail?

I try to restrict what I do to the important things. I concentrate on strategy, i.e. identifying the direction we should be moving in.

A lot of my job is generating ideas. I may not always be in the office, but I think about the business a lot of the time.

I see myself like one of those people who do the spinning plates on a pole. I keep all the plates spinning. I hold the business together, keep it moving and keep it motivated.

At the end of the day, my desk is clean and that's how it should be. I am available to sort out problems and as I am the person in the company with the most experience, I am pretty useful in a crisis. It would worry me, though, if problem-solving were all I did, because that would be a symptom of lack of management further down the line.

I see myself as a coach for the business. I push people, I guide and help them. I bounce ideas off them.

As I am very involved in the day-to-day running of the company and as traditionally the role of chairman is seen as being more involved with external relationships and strategy, I have taken the title of managing director. Unfortunately, a public image presents many pitfalls. I'm reluctant to be seen as the public face of Richer Sounds when this really is a team effort. It would also be galling for my colleagues if I were to give interviews everywhere when the success of the company is really down to us all pulling together. It would be against our culture of a close-knit team working together.

I have found the press are usually interested in the 'long-haired millionaire' story, when what I really want to talk about is the culture of the business, which is much more important and really much more interesting. That is why I wrote this book in the first place.

I aim to lead from the front and I expect all my managers to do the same. In most businesses it's 'us and them'. Senior management are all chummy with each other and they don't like to get their hands dirty. They treat the junior staff with contempt. I have no time for companies that have a luxury directors' dining room for 'us' and a canteen for 'them', where the food is rubbish but the bosses don't care because, after all, they don't have to eat there.

I was horrified to visit a supplier's factory in China many years ago where this was taken to extremes. There were three canteens: one for senior managers, one for middle managers and one for junior staff that did not even have tables and chairs – they had to eat standing up. The senior managers did the utmost (unsuccessfully) to prevent me eating in the works canteen. And all this in a socialist country to boot!

In my company it's just the opposite. My senior managers don't disappear in the afternoon for a spot of golf. They are under enormous pressure and really have to lead from the front. I am relatively easy on our junior staff. When something goes wrong, it is the senior managers who have to carry the can. That is what they get paid for.

7

Customer service

Everybody knows these days that customer service is important. This applies not only to commercial enterprises that obviously depend on their customers spending money with them, but also increasingly to services, including public services like schools and hospitals, where people do not pay on the spot.

So I am amazed how little has been written about customer service. In fact, I suspect few organisations have given any systematic thought to what constitutes good service and how you achieve it. For too many organisations, good customer service is an afterthought, an optional extra to their 'real' business of selling saucepans or being a bank. To the customer, however, the service is a fundamental part of the experience of buying that product or interacting with that company.

Good or bad service affects us personally and I think this has not been sufficiently acknowledged.

We all know how it feels to go to a restaurant with good food and pleasant décor, but have the whole evening spoilt by rotten service.

It often happens that we are treated dismissively or rudely by someone serving us and the incident rankles for hours, if not days. Furthermore, we tell our friends about it and nearly everyone has at least one tale to tell about dreadful service – often dating back years.

Why is customer service so important to us? The relationship between the customer and the server is a human relationship like any other and, as the customer, we need to feel that attention is being paid to us. Just as in any relationship, it is important to our feeling of well-being that we are treated with respect. When the clerk or sales assistant talks to a colleague all the time they are serving us, when they patronise us or refuse to take our demands seriously, we feel slighted and threatened.

The implications of this are far-reaching. A significant part of our personal contacts every day are as customers, even if it is only buying a newspaper or a bus ticket. Every time we are treated with friendliness and respect we feel better for it. The sales assistant or service provider also feels good if they've been appreciated. I'm sure that if customer service improved, the world would be a happier place!

It is no good 'discovering' customer service and then thinking you can introduce it into your organisation by sending front-line staff on a three-day training course. The whole organisation has to be dedicated to serving the customer. The company organisation chart we give to our new recruits at Richer Sounds clearly shows the customer at the apex of the pyramid. The customer is simply the most important person we deal with. If the customer is not being served well, we are not doing our jobs properly and the company will not survive.

I have always taken customer service seriously. I suppose it is part of my philosophy that people should be treated with respect. Even in my first shop, we always made a point of addressing customers as 'sir' or 'madam'. For a lot of our customers, who were often students, or at least not exactly flush with money, this courtesy was a novelty, but they liked it.

People now expect better service. US companies, or British companies that have learnt from the States, have raised their standards. So expectations are rising and everyone has to work harder to excel. However, I think a lot of British businesses have yet to make the fundamental change of attitude needed to deliver great customer service. There has to be that shift away from regarding the customer as a nuisance who gets in the way of doing the job, to an attitude of total commitment to putting the customer first.

What is good customer service?

Customer service is an inexact science and everyone will have different views on what constitutes good service. Views also change all the time and expectations rise. So these are purely my personal feelings, based on experience both as a retailer and as a customer myself. I have given a lot of thought to customer service and I have not yet found a better definition than the following. If you have a better definition, let me know.

I see good customer service as a combination of three things: product, procedures and people.

Firstly, it is the integrity of the product itself. Its design, build quality, reliability and serviceability all must be of the standard the customer wants and needs. It must do what it is supposed to do. This applies as much to services as to products.

Saying 'Have a nice day' as the customer walks off with a dress that will fall apart the first time she washes it, or an insurance policy that will not provide sufficient cover, is not good service.

Secondly, there is the integrity of your procedures. You can have the best products on the market, but if they are not on the shelf, not available in the sizes people want, not priced, beyond their sell-by date or customers have to queue for half an hour to buy them, you are not giving good service.

The same applies to services, especially public services, which often simply do not reach the people supposed to be benefiting from them. Customers have to hang on the telephone for ages, queue, get on waiting lists, even go to a Citizens Advice Bureau or petition their MP – just to get access to some services.

The third element in good customer service is the quality of the experience. You cannot give good service without friendly, helpful, knowledgeable people. It's all very well having a great product, but if the people selling it or providing it are miserable and surly, that cannot be described as good customer service.

This book is not about the products so I won't talk about production or design. I'm talking about the other two elements – the procedures and the friendliness of the experience – as there are principles here that apply no matter what the product.

Good customer service has to have all three elements, but there is not really a formula for success. You have to respond to each individual customer's needs and every customer is different.

In my company, I want not just good, but legendary, customer service. I want examples of service that will be talked about for years afterwards, like the time one of our staff wrote out an entire instruction manual for a customer who couldn't wait for it to be ordered from the manufacturer. Or when our Liverpool store relocated and the team carried out the whole move, including refitting the new shop and moving all the stock. They did this between the old shop closing on Saturday evening and the new one opening for business on Monday morning, so that there was absolutely no disruption for customers.*

The point about customer service is that it is hard work and it never ends. You can give brilliant service to 100 people, but that's not going to impress the 101st that gets treated badly.

Why is good customer service so important?

Will good customer service really make a difference to your business? Yes, for four reasons.

Good customer service is the cheapest and most effective form of advertising

When you read the Sunday papers you read dozens of advertisements. By Monday morning

---

* This was obviously before Sunday trading!

you can remember very few of them. But if you meet friends in the pub on a Sunday evening who tell you about this great hi-fi and TV store, where the staff were tremendous, you'll remember and you might call into the branch next time you are passing.

A word-of-mouth recommendation is always more convincing and is much better value than advertising.

The other side of the coin is that if people tell their friends about good service, they are even more likely to regale them with stories of bad service. Think of those 400 people hearing complaints about you for every one you hear directly and ask yourself if you can afford *not* to give good service.

Customer service is a differentiating factor

How do customers choose to buy from you and not from the competition? One of the reasons should be the service they get. This is especially important if what you are selling is not very different from other companies' products. You can buy a tin of baked beans in any one of twenty supermarkets, at much the same price. The only thing that varies is the way the product is sold to you.

The environment is also a factor. A friendly environment is an essential part of good customer service, though décor and style are less important.

People enjoy being served in a pleasant place and the environment certainly sends a message as to how that organisation values its customers, but people do not like the surroundings to count for more than the service. Customers will often say that they find luxurious offices and shops intimidating. Employees are also resentful if you spend more on the fixtures and fittings than you do on them.

Good service makes people come back

You can attract people into buying your product or service with special offers and deals. However, price advantages can only ever be short term, so good service should be your 'conversation tool' to turn those new customers into loyal, long-term customers.

In fact, there is no point in having a promotion or sale unless you are ready to offer amazing service that will make those customers want to come back.

The danger with just relying on price is that people will graze from bargain to bargain and will not return to you if they can find a cheaper deal elsewhere. A good example is that if you move into a new area and want to get your car serviced or your hair cut, you might well phone round the local garages or hairdressers to see who seems to offer the best deal. Once you pick one, if you receive excellent service from your car mechanic or hairdresser, you will go straight back there next time and not bother phoning around.

Good service prompts impulse buying

When you go shopping for entertainment, as many people do, you are much more likely to buy something that catches your eye if you are served by a smiling, attentive sales assistant than by an indifferent teenager chewing gum. Good service can make all the difference between whether a customer makes a purchase or not.

Some businesses feel they can only offer either good prices or good service and they are not able – or willing – to do both. The unspoken argument is: if customers want good service they will have to pay for it.

Well, good service ought to be the foundation of the whole business, so why should customers pay extra? Secondly, customers don't like paying extra for service. It is very difficult to persuade the guests in a five-star hotel that the service is outstanding, as they know they are paying a lot of money and expect a service to match.

My views on customer service are obviously based on my own experience in competitive retail markets. If you are a monopoly supplier, does that mean you need to worry about pleasing customers because they have nowhere else to go? Too many organisations seem to take this attitude – utilities in particular, perhaps – but since the government has opened up many areas to competition their poor service has backfired. Look at the outcry over British Gas when it was revealed that customer complaints were rising even faster than its top management's salaries. They lost many customers to new, alternative suppliers because they were looking not just for cheaper prices but also quality of service.

What separates the real winners from the losers is providing great value for money together with great customer service. I see value for money as a combination of quality and price – 'quality per £', as I describe it.

Responsibility for quality comes down to your professional skills, your manufacturing processes or your buying team, depending on what sort of product or service you offer. Getting the right price depends both on your efficiency and your judgement of the market. With experience, it is possible to get both quality and price right.

Customer service is very different. Responsibility for it lies in the hands of all of the employees who come into contact with the customer. In many cases these will be your most junior staff, perhaps working unsupervised. Yet every person who deals with the customer is an ambassador for the entire organisation. Your organisation will be judged on the performance of that individual.

So the potential for getting it wrong is enormous. Even if you have recruited and trained people as best you can, employees are fallible. They have days off, they make mistakes, and customers can come forward with unforeseeable problems.

I certainly haven't found a way of eliminating mistakes. Our catalogue used to carry the following warning to our customers: 'Due to recent changes in government legislation, our lawyers tell us that it is necessary to employ human beings in our stores. Although we think they are the best you'll find, please don't expect the impossible.'

One of the basic principles of my approach to customer service is to under-promise and over-deliver.

This starts as soon as someone walks into one of our shops. They look at a small store stacked high with equipment and probably think, 'What a bunch of cowboys.' When they find out that we're knowledgeable, professional and do our best to give great service, they are doubly impressed.

In the same way, I tell my staff not to promise too much. If a customer asks how long a repair will take and you say a week, then if it takes ten days you'll have an irate customer ringing you up. If you say three weeks and it arrives in ten days, the customer will be delighted.

Companies that advertise thirty-point service pledges are digging a big pit for themselves. It is not possible to live up to them every time and, as soon as you slip up, you will have customers demanding a refund. There are also the professional complainers who seem to make a living out of looking for mistakes.

Don't make customer service your big marketing pitch. Many businesses are doing themselves no favours by the over-the-top claims to great service they make in their advertising. Banks and building societies seem to be the worst at this. They may have the best of intentions, but the ad agencies who dream up their stylish advertisements making these huge claims do not appear to realise that they are simply handing customers a stick with which to beat their clients. Good service advertises itself in much better ways – through word of mouth.

How to give great service

The real question is how do you deliver? How do you get your staff to give the extra that turns a reasonable service into a great service?

Management commitment

Organisations will never achieve legendary customer service if the management does not really believe in it. I am not talking about standing up at the Christmas dinner and saying how wonderful customer service is. I mean living and breathing it, ensuring that the entire organisation is driven by the desire to give good service.

It also means allocating resources. Good service costs money. I would argue that it is money you cannot afford not to spend.

Recruiting and training the right people

If you want good service, recruit the kind of people who are most likely to give it. Are your staff the kind of people you would like to be served by?

Training is obviously paramount. In the next chapter I will look more closely at the kind of techniques to use to give good service. You must have the right procedures in your organisations to put good customer service into practice, and people must be trained thoroughly and regularly in those procedures.

Motivation

In writing this book, the reason I dealt with motivation before customer service is that if you do not treat your staff well, they will not treat customers well. Motivation affects everything they do and you need it in place before they even start to serve customers.

I've often been invited to advise companies on customer care, and I always ended up advising them on staff motivation. Good customer service is hard work, sometimes difficult and staff must *want* to do it. Unless they have that motivation as a base, you cannot add customer service on top.

Accountability and measurement

What gets measured gets done. This goes as much for customer service as anything else.

Staff must be accountable. If they give bad service, they must answer for it and if they give excellent service, this should also be identified so it can be recognised and rewarded.

The best way to assess how good the service is is to ask the customer. It is not good service unless the customer thinks so.

At Richer Sounds we have developed effective ways of measuring customer service and holding staff accountable, which are explained in more detail in the next chapter.

A customer-friendly environment

Whatever your office or shop is like, it should be welcoming to customers. This covers many things:

ease of access, the state of the décor, the layout of the space.

It also means the way employees greet customers and talk to them. It even means the messages you convey through your signs. Many shops are unfriendly to the point of being hostile, for example, 'no smoking', 'no eating', 'no change given', 'no directions', 'no schoolchildren', 'no dogs', even 'no boots' (usually in the Yorkshire Dales or other walking country) and 'shoplifters will be prosecuted'. Then, if you still want to enter, 'the management takes no responsibility for what happens to you'!

Richer Sounds shops have a sign up inviting people in to ask for directions, browse around or just shelter from the rain. We want people inside our shops. Everyone who comes in is a potential customer. That's my recipe for creating great customer service. At Richer Sounds we try to follow this programme and although we don't always get it right, we know this approach can work. Over the years we have refined our techniques for giving great service and, while they have been developed for a retail environment, you might find something useful in them whatever your type of organisation.

8

If good customer service was easy, everyone would be doing it

Giving great customer service is hard work. It takes training, effort and the ability to learn from experience.

Unless they are motivated, most people at work will do the minimum to get by. Giving great customer service means doing the maximum for the customer, so that customers go home enthusing, 'Their staff were marvellous, they couldn't do enough for me!'

Real customer service is about adapting to the individual customer. To give good service you have to tune into people, listen to what they are saying and respond. Make them always the centre of attention.

Every customer service situation is different and that is what makes it difficult to control. It is also what makes serving the public exciting and fun.

That doesn't mean you leave front-line staff to make it up as they go along, though. Following our *kaizen* principle, we have tried to identify the best way of handling every situation. Our procedures have been developed from experience, and improved on. We have looked at the whole process under a microscope, examining every moment of customer contact and thinking about how best to serve them at that point.

This does mean we have a lot of procedures for staff to learn, and it is not easy for them. There has to be a commitment to training. They learn what works, they are measured on what they do and they are then rewarded.

We draw in the detail, but we don't want to turn our employees into robots. We don't give them a script so that every customer gets exactly the same lines.

You must make the customer feel special and to do that you need different techniques up your sleeve, to be able to deal with different situations. Training must give staff the tools to do their job and they then must have the initiative to decide which tools are right for that situation.

Friendly places

In customer service, first impressions have a disproportionate importance. People decide within seconds whether they are in a friendly or a hostile environment. Start with the messages you are sending customers before they have exchanged a word with your staff.

I once visited a superstore that had been given a multimillion-pound refurbishment. The first sign that greeted me when I walked in the main entrance was a yellow warning triangle on a door showing a stick man lying on the ground with a thunderbolt through him, accompanied by the words: 'danger of death'. What this actually meant was that if you smashed through the two locks on the door, broke into the switch room and stuck your finger in one of the machines, you could electrocute yourself. It seemed rather unnecessary and was not much of a welcome.

Instead of all those 'no' signs you see everywhere ('no dogs', 'no smoking'), it is much better to convey the same message in a positive way. Stating that 'guide dogs are welcome' also implies that other dogs are not.

Many shops have big signs saying, 'Shoplifters will be prosecuted.' I have never heard of these actually deterring a thief. In some of our shops we have a fun sign: 'Free ride in a police car – for shoplifter's today only.' It makes the same point and, perhaps more usefully, it makes the honest customers laugh.

We like amusing signs because we think that if we can get customers to smile, we are halfway there. As most of our stores are in town centres, parking is usually a problem for customers. We dish out free cards from dispensers on the shop windows for them to put on their windscreen saying, 'Dear traffic warden, I've just popped to Richer Sounds. PS I think traffic wardens are wonderful!' Can this really get round a hardened traffic warden? It's worth a try.

Think about how customers will get into your shop or office. It is obvious that organisations whose customers are likely to be pushing a baby buggy, or are elderly or disabled, need to think about whether they can get in at all without extreme difficulty.

In Britain customers tend to be shy and they can even be reluctant to push open a door. We got rid of doors in our shops* so there are no barriers to people just wandering in. We simply have security shutters we pull down at night. Admittedly, this can make it a bit cold for staff in the winter, so we combat this with heaters over the doorways and company-issue thermal underwear for the sales assistants.

What about the layout of space? Are things easy and logical to find? Do the labels carry the information customers want? Is everything clearly priced?

* They're going back on again now due to pollution.

Point-of-sale material also sends a big message. It should be friendly to customers as well as trying to sell. Staff usually have good ideas about what kind of point-of-sale works and we have had plenty of useful ideas come through the suggestion scheme about this.

There is so much you can do to make a place welcoming. We have hot drinks machines in all the stores free of charge for customers. We also have freezers full of ice lollies in the summer and a ready supply of lollipops all year round. And these aren't just for the kids. We give them out to everyone on the grounds that if a customer is in a bad mood, they are going to feel a bit silly trying to scream at us with a lolly in their mouth.

These giveaways really do not cost very much. In fact, for us the most expensive item is the space taken up by the drinks machines in our small shops. And they are available as much to the browser as to the person spending £1,000. The message is that all our customers are special to us.

At Christmas we give out mince pies (though not after Boxing Day because people are sick of the sight of them by then) and hot cross buns at Easter. Over the summer Bank Holiday weekend we have also handed out sticks of rock as a small compensation for all those families who thought they were going to have a nice day out at the beach and instead found themselves being dragged round hi-fi and TV stores.

Rainy days are some of our busiest times, but no one likes shopping when it is raining so we started giving out free umbrellas to customers.

Another useful little item we give away is tape measures. It's amazing how few customers know the size of the shelves at home where they will be putting their new system.

Going on stage

Everyone who deals with a customer is taking the role of representative for the entire organisation. When employees walk onto the shop or office floor, they are going on stage.

Presentation is very important. At Richer Sounds we are quick to comment if staff look scruffy. We don't expect our employees to be models of physical perfection, but we do expect them to be clean and tidy. A mirror in the staffroom is an absolute must.

Given that they will be standing close to customers, we also make sure they attend to their personal freshness and are not breathing the remnants of last night's curry over the poor shopper. We even put it in the contract of employment that no one is to eat things like garlic and onions less than twelve hours before working in a store.

Appearance does matter. Looking smart gives you confidence and it also gives the customer confidence in you.

Approaching the customer

In the retail business, this is probably the most difficult and delicate part of the whole process of dealing with the customer.

The British do not like sales assistants to be over-friendly – they see it as pushy – but then customers get just as annoyed if they feel they are being ignored.

So we have devised ways of giving customers our attention without hassling them. To begin with, never make a beeline for customers. Take the indirect approach. We train our staff to look busy – they do some dusting or adjust a few catalogues close to the customer, then say casually, 'Are you ok there?' or 'Are you happy browsing, sir/madam?' Customers then feel pleased the sales assistant has noticed them.

The approach to the customer is not an attempt to sell them anything. It is simply to make eye contact and to let the customer know you are aware of their presence and that they can contact you when they are ready.

We have signs on our stores saying 'Browsers welcome' and we mean it. They won't feel welcome if we hassle them.

As I said earlier, the words not to use at this point are: 'Can I help you?' This almost always elicits a negative answer. The customer then does not know what to say when they are no longer looking and want some service. It is much better to ask a question to which they reply with a 'yes'.

Some customers of course know what they want and march straight up to the counter. Again, I prefer to avoid the question 'Can I help you?' because it never really sounds friendly and, anyway, it is redundant. It is much simpler to smile and say, 'Good afternoon.'

It is also important to acknowledge the customer even if you are busy at the counter and cannot approach them. The French have a wonderful way of simply saying '*bonjour*' to everyone who walks in the shop. It is worth trying a straightforward greeting (in English!) like that.

Customers should only be approached once. So if you have several sales assistants on the floor, you don't want each of them in turn asking the customer if they are OK. In our shops we have a code to prevent this occurring. Instead of one assistant whispering to another to find out if they have spoken to that customer, they ask, 'Have you done the window?' to which the reply will be something like, 'I have done that window, but not that one.' The customers are oblivious to the fact that the assistants are talking about them.

Once you have approached a customer and they are happy browsing, don't stand in a row with your other sales colleagues behind the counter staring at them. Women know how unnerving it is in fashion stores where they run the gamut of teenage sales assistants, all whispering and giggling together. The sales staff should split up, look purposeful and generally create a friendly, busy environment.

What happens when you are very busy and customers have to queue? Personally, I hate it when the assistant makes me wait while they finish a phone call or serve the person in front of me and then turn to me, apparently oblivious to the fact that I have been standing there for ten minutes, with a curt, 'Who's next?'

So be attentive to customers queuing. All waiting customers should be acknowledged. The sales assistant should not just concentrate on the one person they are serving, ignoring everyone else. Acknowledging the people queuing has two advantages. Firstly, it sends a subtle message to the person at the front that they should hurry up a little. They might not have realised there was a queue behind them. Secondly, customers who have been acknowledged then feel normally bound to wait.

I have never seen a customer who has been acknowledged walk out of the queue.

When you finally serve the people who have been queuing, always apologise that they had to wait. Simply saying 'Thank you for waiting' or 'Sorry to keep you' is a wonderful way of getting your relationship with the customer on a good footing. It is friendly and polite, and lets the customer know that they are being looked after.

Tune in to the customer

The interesting work starts when you engage the customer in a dialogue.

Every customer is different, has different requirements and they will often surprise you. The trick is to banish stereotypes from your mind and not jump to conclusions about what the customer wants or how much they can afford. Observe them and listen to them as an individual.

In a business like mine, the typical customer is male and under the age of fifty, but we must not assume that a customer over fifty knows nothing about hi-fi, or that if a man and a woman walk in together, it is the man who is going to do the buying.

We also tell staff not to make assumptions based on the way people are dressed. The shabbiest-looking customers might have a gold credit card in their pocket. Or else, the customer might really not be well-off, in which case they should be treated even more nicely, because for them a £150 purchase could be a very big decision. Beauty is only skin deep, a customer's spending power isn't even that!

You also have to provide the same quality of service to the customers who are pompous, flashy, aggressive, rude or boring. This is where it becomes a challenge. Anyone can serve a friendly, easy-going customer, but if you can handle a belligerent or negative person and turn them round into someone who is delighted with the service, that is a real professional achievement. Some people seem sceptical and resist being 'sold to', but if you can satisfy them, they can be among your best advertisers for the business.

Staff should not patronise customers. We have all been served by people who manage to convey that they are not really clerks or shop assistants, but brain surgeons taking a little holiday job and that this kind of work is actually far beneath them.

Don't get competitive with customers either. Whatever they are buying, don't tell them you have got one twice as good at home and if they say they've just got back from Mallorca don't tell them you went to the Seychelles this year. They haven't come to you to feel small.

The sale

There are hundreds of books about selling techniques, and very many of them seem to start from the premise that selling means cornering the customer and persuading them to buy something against their will.

I cannot think of anything worse than pushing people into buying something they do not really want. That is incredibly short-term thinking. Above all, we want our customers to be happy with what they buy from us and to come back in the future.

If we're serious about customer service, we should not need to ram our goods down customers' throats. The integrity of the product should speak for itself.

The whole selling operation should be transparent. There should be no pressure, no trying to disguise a duff product, no catches. The product should work and the customers should be happy with it – if not they should get their money back.

We do not have a sales league. The sales commission should be a good enough incentive for our staff to want to sell as much as they can. However, we do monitor their commission because we want to make sure they are out there serving customers, not lounging around in the staffroom.

Each store has a bespoke target agreed between my CEO and each individual store manager reflecting the intention of that particular store. Many stores that have had a good year won't see their target increase, while poor-performing stores (luckily very few!) might have increases of up to 1000 per cent!

While we are exacting on customer service, we are fairly relaxed about selling techniques. Apart from telling them to be confident and not pushy, we leave it up to the sales assistant to develop their own style.

We give them lots of suggestions and ideas, for example on how to sell warranties, but they are not expected to parrot set phrases at the customer. It's more of a partnership: we explain some ways to sell, but they can use them as they wish. We never check word for word what they have said.

Our training manual is a very detailed document and looks pretty daunting. It is the product of years of experience and tries to cover every eventuality in the shop. It sets out procedures that must be followed, together with some common-sense principles to remember. All of it is designed to produce great service.

The sales procedure will vary depending on what kind of product or service you are providing, but I believe the following points apply to most situations.

Tell the truth

It is vital not to bullshit customers. You are building a relationship that must be based on trust, so never lie to them. Customers will often test you at first, by asking questions they know the answer to. They are sounding you out to see if you are trustworthy.

Never forget that you are selling integrity as well as a product. If you show integrity, the customer will trust you and will buy again from you. If you do not have integrity, the customer will soon find out.

So if you don't know the answer to a technical query, don't try to bluff your way through. Honesty is the best policy. Simply say, 'I'm sorry I don't know, but I can find out', and then go and find the answer.

Don't swap sell

If a customer asks for something, give it to them unless there is an ethical reason not to. I hate it when sales assistants transparently try to swap sell – telling me I should buy a different model because the one I am interested in is 'unreliable'. As I've said before, it hardly inspires confidence in a business if it appears to be selling poor quality goods. It also shows that the sales assistant has taken no notice of the customer's particular requirements.

If you can't make the sale, still give the service

Sometimes customers ask for things we don't stock. We always keep copies of Argos and Maplin catalogues behind the counter so that we can see if the customer can find what they want elsewhere. This is a nice customer service touch. Time and again I have seen customers, after they have been helped in this way, stop and think before they walk out to see if they can buy anything else from us to show their appreciation.

Under-promise, over-deliver

This is the most important piece of customer service advice, combined with 'Do what you say you will do.'

It is always tempting to promise customers the moon just to make a sale, but your long-term relationship with the customer will be damaged when they find out you can't deliver.

This even applies to tiny things such as what you say on the phone. Don't ask people to hang on for 'two seconds' when you know it will be more like a minute.

Be patient and friendly

It can be difficult to be patient when you are busy, but customers try your patience even more during quiet times. Patience and friendliness cost nothing and are the signs of a real customer service champion. Customers will sense very quickly if you are irritated by them. By all means, when the shop or office gets suddenly busy, take control of the situation and be more assertive with customers to speed them up, but do it without being stroppy.

Friendliness is by far the most important quality in anyone dealing with the public. Customers will accept an awful lot from friendly people.

I have often talked with or read letters from customers who have had a problem with an item bought from our shops, but they are pleased, saying things like, 'The sales assistant was so helpful, they sorted it out straight away.' It is clear that a customer's initial anger at finding a problem is easily outweighed by their delight at encountering friendliness and helpfulness.

Closing the sale

It is crazy to push customers into buying something they are not sure they want. At best they will feel resentful and at worst they will vow never to return and tell all their friends too.

If customers are not sure about a purchase, our staff are instructed to tell them NOT to buy it. We advise customers to go away and think about it, discuss it with their partner or do some more research.

This works wonders. The message we are sending is one of the supreme confidence in our products. We are not desperate to sell. This gives the customer confidence too and seems to be the factor that tips them into making the decision to purchase. Sometimes they browse around the shop a little and then decide, sometimes they come back later in the day or a few days later. They have made their decision themselves and feel good about it.

The sales assistant's role is to stimulate the customer's desire for the product, not to bully them into taking it. Telling the customer to think about it is a very effective way to stimulate that desire.

You won't find many books on selling techniques advising this approach, because most of these books are not written with customer service in mind.

If the customer thinks about it and decides not to purchase, that is not a failure. The long-term relationship with the customer is more important than the immediate sale because we want their custom for life. We make sure that they leave at least with a quote form, reminding them of the model and price. We aim to create the right conditions to prompt them to come back in the future.

Handling hagglers

One of my pet hates when travelling by plane is people who demand an upgrade. There's nothing more annoying when you've paid full price for your club-class ticket to find someone is demanding the seat next to you at economy price. Upgrades and two-tier pricing in general may make sense from a short-term revenue point of view, but they add up to very poor customer service. Why should someone who turns up at the last minute have a product (an airline seat, a holiday, a page of advertising or whatever) much cheaper than the person who books in advance and pays money upfront? Customers dislike this. Why should better customers subsidise other travellers?

Many years ago I knew a chief executive of a large business who told me he sits in first class on a plane when he doesn't have a first-class ticket. He nearly always got away with it. I have to say it makes my blood boil! From a customer service point of view it's very unfriendly to give people favours just because they muscle in. I lose respect for those companies that do not have the courage to treat everyone the same.

So two-tier pricing is not as clever as some people think. At Richer Sounds we don't give discounts to minority groups, i.e. students, OAPS, civil servants, etc., and we don't barter. We often get hagglers and customers who insist on having some sort of discount. Their argument is usually that they are spending a lot of money, or paying cash, or buying the last item on display, and so on.

If someone has seen the product cheaper elsewhere, we will always beat the competition because we want the business, but most of the time we are confident our prices are the best.

It is easy to 'buy' a good relationship with the customer by giving them something for free or a big discount, but this is a short-term attitude. We would rather lose a sale than acquire a reputation for customers naming their price: it makes us look desperate.

We occasionally give special offers through magazines, but on the whole retailers who are always offering deals are doing their product no good at all. If you've just spent a lot of money on a new kitchen and two weeks later you see the same shop selling kitchens marked down by 40 per cent in some sort of spring (or summer, autumn or winter) offer, you feel very bad. You think the shop has made a fool of you, the customer.

The job of the buyers is to make sure they are obtaining the best price for everyone all the time. There's nothing worse for your decent, regular customers than to see you giving the best price to the person who shouts the loudest.

We have to be careful about how we refuse, though. Rejecting the customer outright could damage the relationship. We say something like, 'You are quite right to ask, sir/madam ... but I'm afraid we are not allowed to as our prices are already cut to the bone. I can throw in a few bits and pieces, though.' And then we may include a few accessories.

We have to strike a balance. We believe we give good value and it is important to have clear prices in the store. We don't want to end up like a market. On the other hand, if people are spending a lot of money with us, we appreciate that and do not want to offend them.

Payment manners

Forgeries are a real problem these days, but it is humiliating for the customer to hand over their cash and then stand there while the assistant holds every note up to the light. When it happens to me, I find that the lower the value the note, the worse I feel. Do I really look like the sort of bloke who passes on dud fivers?

All you have to do is explain politely that you have been asked to check notes. Think how you would feel if the customer pointedly examined the notes in their change.

The same goes when counting cash. Anyone handing you a wad of £20 notes should be a valued customer, so be pleasant about it and make a comment like, 'I just want to check you haven't given me too much.'

Some shops make a great fuss if you try to pay for a small item by credit card. We tell our staff that a battery customer today is a hi-fi customer tomorrow, so don't make them more embarrassed than they already are by putting on a martyred air when letting them pay by credit card.

I vividly recall paying for a meal in a restaurant I had patronised for twenty years. I used a credit card that, unknown to me, had been prematurely cancelled by the issuer, pending a replacement that was still in the post. I ended up in the embarrassing position of having the manager confiscate my card in front of dozens of nosy diners, then having to argue on the phone and try to convince them they had made a mistake – to no avail. I felt outraged at being unjustly accused and I went home and made a sizeable donation to Amnesty.

The moral of that story is that mistakes do happen and just because a credit card is not accepted does not mean you have caught the mastermind of a fraud ring.

How can I do better?

Similar to *kaizen* in operational matters, after each transaction, or even conversation, with the customer, look back and think how you could have improved it. What more could I have done to help the customer? Why did I get irritated? Did that affect the transaction? How can I learn from that? This is the mark of true dedication to customer service.

The last minute

How often have you gone into a shop and been served by a really friendly and enthusiastic sales assistant, only to find that as soon as they have taken your money, they switch off from you completely and turn to the next customer?

This happened to me once and I felt as if I had been conned. Thinking about it afterwards, I realised this was because I felt vulnerable after I had parted with my cash. We make at least part of our buying decision on the advice of the sales assistant, because we trust them. When this charm is so visibly switched off as soon as we have made the purchase, we feel cheated and foolish.

So it is vital to follow the service through until the customer is out of the shop. In fact, it is especially important to be attentive at this point when the customer is feeling vulnerable. Last impressions count.

There are many ways in which you can make the closing minutes with the customer pleasant ones. Thank them for their custom, give them your name to contact if there are any problems, say goodbye and even perhaps help them to their car.

A final nice touch if the customer is uncertain about the purchase, is to offer what we call a CHC – a customer happy call. Offer to take the customer's phone number and call them in a few days to check that they are happy with their purchase. We also print on the receipt that we may ask for the customer's phone number for this purpose, to reassure them that this is above board.

Using the telephone

At Richer Sounds we define answering the phone as one of the most important jobs in the shop, second only to serving customers face-to-face who are in the process of purchasing.

The telephone is a key customer service tool. All phone calls should be treated as though they are from potential new customers, so they are an opportunity to impress the caller with your friendliness and helpfulness.

Your voice on the line creates the total picture of the business and you must remember this throughout the conversation.

The telephone is also obviously a selling tool. If someone rings us with an enquiry, we concentrate on getting them to come into the shop so that we don't lose them to a competitor.

The telephone should be answered as quickly as possible and we give our staff instructions on telephone protocol. If the phone is ringing while you are serving a customer and there is no one else around to answer it, the rule is to ask the customer if they mind you answering the phone.

Apart from anything else, this is good manners. It is rude to ignore the person in front of you and rush off to answer the phone.

Companies will have their own policy on what to say on answering the phone. What is even more important is your tone of voice. It is not what you say, it's the way you say it that sends a message to the caller.

We test our shops on this by doing a telephone survey every fortnight. The item that counts for the most points is the friendliness of the person answering.

If you get a long-winded telephone call during a busy period, you can suggest taking their number and calling them back at a quieter moment, but if you promise this, then you must make sure you do it.

Customers might come up to the counter while you are on the phone and it is important to acknowledge them. We provide our staff with a table tennis bat with the message on it, 'Sorry to keep you – won't be a moment', so that they need not interrupt the phone call.

I have to admit that perfect telephone procedures are not easy. I was once travelling round Ireland with Feargal Quinn (the president of Irish supermarket chain Superquinn) and Archie Norman (then chairman of Asda) in Feargal's car. To demonstrate our fantastic telephone service, I eagerly phoned one of our branches. The phone rang and rang – and rang. In the end I mumbled something about having a wrong number and quickly phoned another branch. To my intense relief they answered immediately. My friends were not fooled and teased me mercilessly about it.

Encouraging complaints

It would be nice to say that if you follow all my customer service suggestions, you won't receive any complaints. Sorry, but it is a fact of life that things go wrong and people complain.

The good news is that you should welcome complaints. If you think about the statistic that there could be 400 unhappy customers for every one who complains to you, the best way to tackle this is to get people to complain more readily. If you know about their problem, you can sort it out. The people you should worry about are all the ones who don't like to complain, but moan to their friends instead.

If a customer complains to us, we do at least still have a relationship with them and that is far better than their simply going to another shop. We can also learn. Only when people tell us what we have done wrong can we put it right. And someone who has had their complaint dealt with to their satisfaction can become a very loyal customer.

So all organisations should encourage complaints with a passion. Once you do, of course you get more complaints, but don't be discouraged. It does not mean that the customers are necessarily more dissatisfied – it just means that you hear about it more often.

We get a lot of complaints at Richer Sounds and sometimes people are shocked that we admit that. If a company claims to have no complaints, it is by no means proven that they are giving good service. They can't possibly know if they're giving good service unless they invite people's views – and some of those views are bound to be complaints.

I estimate that of every three people who are unhappy with Richer Sounds, one or two complain directly to us. So the ratio between the complaints we receive and the number of people who hear bad things about us drops to, at worst, 1:60.

The British, being terribly polite, are often reluctant to complain and prefer to suffer in silence, so you have to make it easy for them. You should aim to get complaints early on, before a problem turns into a disaster.

We have divided the customer interface into smaller and smaller segments, and made sure that at every stage the customer has the opportunity to come back to us. So at every point where something could go wrong, there is a safety valve.

We include a short, tear-off questionnaire on all our receipts (shown in Appendix B). Questionnaires should be brief and to the point – don't expect customers to give up too much of their own time doing something for you – and I also recommend they should be addressed to someone of importance in the organisation, preferably the chief executive. People will be more likely to complain if they feel they can reach someone who can get something done. Ours come to me and we use a freepost address.

Our questionnaires have only eight short questions, including the customer's assessment of the quality of service he or she received, and there is space for their own comments. Needless to say, many write us letters as well.

What if a customer enters a shop, can't find anyone to serve them and walks out in disgust? We have a supply of 'We're listening' cards positioned prominently in a dispenser at the till, which ask customers to let us know what they think of the service they have – or haven't – received.

When people come into our shops to research a purchase, we try not to let them walk out without a quote form, which gives details of the models and prices for comparison purposes. This form also carries an opportunity for them to write to me if they choose not to buy from us, for whatever reason.

We want to hear complaints about repairs and our after-sales service too. We all know sales assistants tend to be nicer to the customer when they are spending money (and earning them commission) than when they are bringing something back.

So we have a repair questionnaire, which asks only four questions. For instance, we ask whether the customer feels the repair was done in an acceptable period of time. It doesn't matter whether it actually took three days or three weeks – what matters is whether the customer was happy with that and whether the period tallied with the time the sales assistant had promised.

Handling complaints

It is not always easy to provide good customer service when an irate customer is facing an exasperated sales assistant and feelings are running high.

Unhappy customers do tend to exaggerate and, as the service provider, we must remember that their perception is the reality. The customer may claim they have been waiting for fifteen minutes when in fact it is only half that time, but the reality is that they feel that they have been waiting far too long.

Never put off dealing with complaints, because when things go wrong they tend to snowball. If you tackle a complaint straight away and take a firm line, you can sort things out before the disgruntled customer takes things further and the next thing you know your company is being featured on *Watchdog*.

People rarely invent complaints, but what can happen is that they get annoyed with a small problem and sometimes blow it up into a big one.

A small proportion of people might be trying to take advantage of you. The difficulty is identifying these to prevent paying out compensation unnecessarily and to protect your staff from unfair accusations. So it is important to hear the employee's side of the story too.

We must give customers the benefit of the doubt when it is their word against ours. However, if we find the same person making regular complaints we have a right to be suspicious!

On the whole, for every one troublemaker there are nineteen genuine complaints that we must treat seriously. We cannot change the rules just because a few people try it on.

So how do you deal with the customer who comes in with all guns blazing? Staff would prefer not to deal with them at all and would much rather serve the nice person waving a credit card than the one with a box under their arm and an angry expression on their face.

The angry customer will only get more annoyed if they are not dealt with promptly. Acknowledge their presence immediately, ask them to put the box on the counter and deal with them as soon as you can. As soon as they start to complain, the first thing to do is to apologise and to listen. Even if you know nothing about the problem or the person did not even buy the goods from your branch, an apology works wonders. The customer has been prepared for battle and resistance. Apologising quickly takes the wind out of their sails.

Once the customer has told their tale, don't fetch the manager and expect the customer to repeat it all over again. Demonstrate that you have been listening by summarising the problem for the manager.

Unless there is a good reason otherwise, our staff are expected to deal with any complaints themselves, and not pass the buck to a senior colleague.

Here are some key things to remember:

- Generosity – if the customer seems to be genuine, be as generous as you can. If they have driven 20 miles to return a DVD player to us, give them a few recordable DVDs for their trouble. This is not supposed to be compensation calculated scientifically, but is rather the sales assistant's own gesture to say sorry.
- Respond quickly – don't say the manager is on holiday for two weeks and you can't do anything until then.
- Independent thinking – make a decision! Complaints handled quickly do not grow into bigger grievances and customers are easier to please at this early stage.
- Be flexible – if the customer wants something a bit out of the ordinary, let them have it.

Typically, a course of action is then agreed on, depending on the nature of the complaint. The key is to follow it through. Make sure the job is done and then followed up with a customer happy call.

There is nothing worse than employees blaming other parts of the company: 'The warehouse is always getting it wrong' or 'The engineers are useless'. This is thoroughly unprofessional and inspires no confidence in the company.

One of the best ways of dealing with a dissatisfied customer is to listen to the complaint, apologise, and say, 'What would you like me to do about it?' This is often the last thing they are expecting you to say and their demands are then usually reasonable. They simply want the item changed or repaired.

If they want their money back, we are happy to do that. Sometimes they are then willing to buy another item from us, because they feel we have treated them fairly.

A good way of dealing with the aggressive customer who 'knows their rights' (but who you know is in the wrong) is to suggest they go to the Citizens Advice Bureau, or even their solicitor. Again, they will not expect you to say this, but it demonstrates the company's confident attitude.

Colleagues who find themselves faced with an unreasonable customer can also advise them to write directly to me. This defuses the situation while the sales assistant can maintain the stance they believe is correct.

It is natural for staff to get emotionally involved, but as a general principle I advise them to stand back and take an objective look at the situation, to try to see it from the customer's point of view, however unpleasant that customer might be.

They sometimes ask me, 'Why do you take the customer's side? Is that being held against us?' The point is that if you care about service, you must give the customer the benefit of the doubt, even if that means customers sometimes get away with false complaints or unreasonable demands. This does not mean the employee should automatically be penalised.

Guarantees are another area where staff can use their initiative. If a customer brings back a faulty item a month after the guarantee has run out, but they appear to have looked after it, the sales assistant has the power to accept the repair under guarantee. Similarly, we offer a fourteen-day exchange, but if someone brings in a machine after three weeks we won't quibble. This generates enormous goodwill because the customer feels we have done something extra for them.

The final point about complaints is to learn from them. We use letters from customers as a training tool and we also put them in our staff magazine (we do publish letters of praise to remind staff that we give good service too).

Measuring customer service

Complaints and compliments are indicators of whether or not you are achieving good customer service, but they are not the only measure.

I want to reward my team for great customer service, so I need to know how each of them has performed. There are various ways of measuring this and I am surprised how many companies say you can't do it. You can.

The questionnaire on our receipt is one of our main tools. We want great service, so while staff receive £5 if the customer ticks the box saying the service was 'excellent', they get nothing for 'good'. A 'mediocre' means a £3 fine and a 'poor' £5. These penalties give the whole system teeth, although in practice we do not make the deductions if they end up with a negative figure at the end of the month.

Our telephone survey also has teeth. The colleague is marked on things such as friendliness and engaging with the customer, and we use real calls from customers to do this. Each observation is worth 25 points, towards a maximum of 100 for which the colleague is paid £10.

For customer service to be measured, clearly staff must be accountable. They must wear name badges and give customers their names on the phone. Colleagues do not need to display their real name or surname if they are concerned about their safety and privacy.

On the receipt questionnaire we do not ask for the salesperson's name as we find customers can be reluctant to complain if they think they are going to get someone into trouble. Instead, the staff member is identified by their payroll number.

It is easy to monitor letters. We also advertise a Freephone number for complaints, so those can be measured too.

The mystery shopper surveys are a good tool we have been using for years. These surveys have to be done regularly to be useful: we have them every two weeks. It can be very sobering to read what an outsider thinks of your service.

The mystery shopper is valuable for giving us information from the public's point of view. We also conduct our own very detailed inspections of each shop, carried out by our store inspectors (not, of course, inspecting their own store). These cover 271 points (at the time of writing), from whether the windows are clean to whether the emergency box contains spare fuses.

All this information is fed into our performance league table, the Richer Way League. Individual colleagues can find out what they earnt in customer service bonuses by checking our internal web system.

Richer's 10 customer service commandments

To summarise, here are my tips for transforming your customer service. These are designed for a retail environment, but most can be adapted to any business or organisation.

1. Get the greeting right. Don't ignore the customer, but don't make them feel hassled either. There is a sensitive balance to achieve.
2. Don't be pushy. If the customer is unsure about the purchase, invite them to go and think about it.
3. Browsers are welcome. People buying batteries or just looking are still important customers and they should have the same quality of service as everyone else.
4. If the item the customer wants is not in stock, suggest where else they can find it, even if that is another retailer.
5. Use the customer's name. And SMILE.
6. Acknowledge customers who are queuing and apologise for keeping them waiting.
7. The last minute spent with the customer is very important. Do everything you can to ensure they leave with a good impression of you.
8. Under-promise and over-deliver. Don't advertise yourself on the basis of your wonderful customer service.
9. Encourage complaints and be grateful for the complaints you receive. Then learn from them.
10. Don't be discouraged when you get it wrong. Keep at it and aim to continually improve.

9
Building a successful business

Treat the people right and the profits will follow. Surely there is more to running a business than motivating your staff and providing good customer service, though? Of course there is, but once you put people first you might find your business priorities are different from those you see in other companies.

Prioritising people means thinking about long-term development rather than short-term gain. It means investing resources in personnel rather than buildings. It means attention to detail, continuous improvement and organic growth.

When I opened my first shop at the age of nineteen I had perhaps a gut instinct about some of these principles, but I hadn't yet worked them out in a systematic way. To begin with, my business was running mainly on raw enthusiasm, but I learnt what worked and, more importantly, why it worked. So I now know a lot more about what makes a successful business.

Starting out

When I was twelve and other kids were into football annuals, I was reading about successful businesspeople and dreaming of having a go myself. I didn't bother with modest ambitions: I had already told my father at that age that I wanted to be financially successful.

Both my parents were in business so I suppose the idea came naturally to me. When I was fourteen my dad suggested I supplement my pocket money by doing a bit of buying and selling.

So I bought a record turntable for £10, did it up and sold it for £22. I made about £10 profit, which in terms of pocket money wasn't bad.

I thought this was great and carried on buying up hi-fi equipment and selling it through *Exchange & Mart* or the local paper. During my school years this built up into a business and by the time I was seventeen I had three people working for me on commission.

As a result, I was offered a job when I left school at a hi-fi shop in London. My parents actually wanted me to be an accountant, but they said I could take a year off and try the shop job.

I was soon the group retail manager running five shops, but I realised I would never be rich working for someone else. I had to find my own business.

I heard about a small shop unit at London Bridge Walk that was coming onto the market and rushed down there to speak to the owner, Vic Odden.

He actually launched my career. I explained to him why I wanted the shop, he listened and must have thought I showed some promise, because not only did he give me the shop premium-free so that I only had to take over the rent, but he said he would lend me £20,000 to start the business. In return he wanted 74 per cent of the shares.

I would also put in the £2,000 I'd saved from my schoolboy wheeling and dealing (all from my original £10 investment) and the idea was that I would buy shares back from him in the course of the years to come.

I actually paid him back within nine months of opening. He took a risk, but did well for himself on the deal. He really gave me my lucky break and we stayed friends to the day he died. He even suggested the 'Richer Sounds' name.

So I started with hi-fi separates and it was a long time until I was confident enough to stray into other product areas. Having tried a lot of different things along the way, I have to say that an important part of business success is finding the right niche market.

The other thing pioneers get is arrows in their backsides. It is rarely the inventors who make the money, unless they have very deep pockets, but the people who come along later and develop the idea commercially. So you don't have to invent something new to start a business. My advice to someone starting out would be to take something that has already been done and improve on it.

Even the most brilliant new ideas take years to get off the ground – video recorders did not become widespread until ten years after they had been invented. It is much easier and safer to take an exciting idea and add value.

The really big business barons have often built their empires on relatively simple commodities. They have succeeded by doing things on a bigger scale, or simply more profitably than their competitors.

So Richer Sounds has developed its own niche. We sell hi-fi separates and few other shops do that. We originally never intended to sell TVs, but as the hi-fi industry has evolved to include home cinema we now sell them so we are able to offer our customers a complete home entertainment package.

So we are specialised. We're a big fish in a small pond and that's how I like it.

The advantage of being an independent retailer is that you can focus on customer service and on developing your staff. This gives you the edge over the high-street chains.

Although I do have to admit that before finding this niche I tried all sorts of things and kept falling flat on my face. One of my first disasters was a telephone shop. Then I went into property and succeeded in losing a lot of money. A friend suggested investing in classic cars so I did, but it was just at the wrong time – at the height of the 1980s boom. More money down the drain.

Selling musical equipment was another failure. I opened a few upmarket hi-fi shops, called Richer Sounds II, but they didn't take off. Neither did Richer Vision, selling TV and video equipment.

Richer Vision had a really clever gimmick. We decided to offer customers a year's free subscription to our video library when they bought a video recorder. The customer somehow failed to see the attraction.

Inevitably, if you try a lot of things some will still go wrong, but even with our failures we try to salvage lessons for the future, to prevent them being repeated.

That does not mean that the original business never changes. We aim to improve constantly and to grow slowly but steadily. We started selling audio-visual equipment (home cinema) and better quality hi-fi, our reference range. To do this we had to transform our shops and find space in them for demonstration rooms. So we're changing, but keeping our new developments closely related to what we already do.

Lessons to learn

My business career has had its ups and downs and I've twice been on the brink of financial disaster. I'm not embarrassed to admit that. In fact, I think the difficult times have taught me the most valuable lessons of all and that I'm now a better businessman for having made those mistakes and pulled through.

In the first few months I kept my London Bridge Walk shop going by buying stock on thirty-day credit and selling it within twenty-five days. Things started to take off when I was offered a job lot of end-of-line cassette decks. They went like hot cakes and I realised I was on to something.

We started to get deals on end-of-line products and, with the right advertising, trade was brisk. Our turnover more than doubled and we began to make a profit.

That is when I started making mistakes. Firstly, we had no accountant, just an unqualified bookkeeper. He estimated we owed £1,500 VAT, when the real figure turned out to be £27,000. Secondly, we did not have specialist auditors. Only when I moved to a West End firm did I find auditors who could advise and help me with the business.

We also had a problem with theft. We did not have good checks and controls and at that point I had a lot to learn about what motivates people. I was letting staff get bored and they started stealing.

The fourth mistake was one made by a lot of inexperienced businesses. Our turnover had rocketed and we thought turnover was profit. I thought we were doing well because a lot of money was going through the till. I had not looked at our profit margins. 'Turnover is vanity, profit is sanity' is worth remembering at times like these.

Finally, I was extravagant. I was twenty-one, it all went to my head, I rushed out and bought a sports car and a flat in Regent's Park and it all came to a sticky end! Halfway through the third year a £20,000 surplus had turned into a £130,000 loss.

Interestingly, I never thought for a moment of giving up. When someone advised me to throw in the towel I was horrified. It had never occurred to me.

With the help of the new auditors, we managed to turn the business round. We first cut the losses to £70,000; the following year we made a profit of £70,000.

It was a tough time. I tightened my belt, sold my flat and stopped taking a salary out of the company for a while. Happily for me, I had met my wife by then, who was very supportive.

Once the business was back on its feet, I began to think about a second shop. We tried another one in London, but that seemed to drain trade from

London Bridge Walk. Then I realised that people were driving down from Manchester to go to London Bridge – so why not open in Manchester?

My knowledge of the north-west was virtually zero but I looked on a map, saw where the motorways went and decided that Stockport looked like the most accessible location.

We made a trip up there and looked round shop units, but nothing seemed suitable. Finally, on the way back to get the train, feeling a bit discouraged, we saw a freehold for sale. It was a tiny street and not exactly upmarket (the only other building on the street was a gents' public toilet), but it was cheap and near the station.

We paid £10,000 for the freehold, stocked up this tiny shop and started advertising. It was a great success. The next step was to open in Birmingham, then Bristol.

Our mistake then was to go from four to sixteen shops in eighteen months. I was undercapitalised and spent too much on expanding. We had grown too quickly and had to cut back. Certain shops were closed and we went back down to eleven stores.

This second difficult period was very different from the first. The problem this time was cash flow. Business was booming, but we didn't have enough money in the kitty to fund our expansion. Cash flow is the fuel that feeds the engines of a business.

So I've nearly lost it twice, but I don't see that as a stigma. I would say it was valuable experience. You learn very fast in a crisis.

You also become stronger. I knew we would survive our second period of trouble because we had come through the first. I learnt what could be achieved and my determination and self-belief increased.

Raising finance

Bank managers are a much maligned group of people, but with careful handling they can be very useful.

The first thing is to find a friendly bank manager. You may think they are all the same, but this is not so. From my experience, if you have ten bank managers in a room and make your business pitch to them, they would all come up with completely different proposals.

This is good news. It means if you have been turned down by several banks, it doesn't mean the next one you see won't take a completely different approach.

I learnt this myself when the business was suffering the cash flow problems after expanding too fast. I went to the bank, with whom I had been for nine years, to ask to extend my overdraft to buy in stock. They would have had the assets of the business and stock as security, which until then had always been good enough for them.

Unfortunately for me, I came up against a new area manager who demanded that I personally guaranteed the entire overdraft. I refused to give personal guarantees and effectively they were saying that after nine years of custom my company wasn't good for a £500 loan unless I were to underwrite it.

My auditors introduced me to another bank, and, in an hour's meeting with the manager, they offered me a very much larger overdraft facility with no personal guarantee.

When I told my original bank I was moving my account they told me it had all been a dreadful mistake and I could have my overdraft, but it was too late. Banks let themselves down because all businesses go through tough times and customers do not forget how they were treated by their banks (or professional advisors or friends) when things were difficult.

In the quest for cash you will probably meet a lot of refusals, but don't get discouraged. Try to find out why you were turned down and how you can improve your presentation next time.

It has to be said that people who lend money are rather conventional and it is no good turning up at a bank in jeans and trainers and expecting to be taken seriously. True, I have long hair and rarely wear a suit – but I can get away with it now because I have a track record.

You have to impress the bank manager with well-prepared profit and loss projections, balance sheets and cash flow forecasts, but you also have to ooze confidence and demonstrate that you really know your business inside and out.

Once you have found a good bank manager, the relationship, like all others in life, needs nurturing. Keep them in the picture about what you are doing and don't give them any nasty surprises.

No one seems to like paying bank charges, but when you are haggling over that last half per cent above base rate, just think how much trouble you had to go to in order to find a decent bank manager. If you are receiving excellent service and support, the peace of mind is worth half a per cent here or there.

Credit controllers are people too

It is strange how people's common sense deserts them when faced with someone to whom they owe money. They will grovel to the bank manager and then breach their overdraft limit because they were too scared to ask for a higher one. They avoid calls from creditors in the vain hope that the unpaid bills will somehow vanish.

What you have to remember is that credit controllers are people too and that they have to make a living. My advice here is that, firstly, everyone has to make a buck, and secondly, what goes around comes around.

What I mean is that it is silly to expect something for nothing. In any deal, both parties must benefit and you cannot begrudge what the other party makes out of the deal, as long as you get what you want out of it.

It pays to know the credit controllers of your various suppliers. When I was dealing with them myself, I always made a point of knowing their names. I used to chat with them on the phone and send them Christmas cards.

If you do have a cash flow problem call the credit controller before it reaches the point where you can't pay your bills. If you talk to them first, they will be more amenable to, say, you sending them a post-dated cheque. If they agree to this, make absolutely sure the cheque doesn't bounce.

Once you have asked for a favour and honoured it, you have proved that you are trustworthy and there will be fewer problems the next time you need their patience. You have to build a relationship.

It never pays to lie or avoid creditors. 'The cheque's in the post', the unsigned cheque or the second-class stamp really are not very clever. You will only get away with that kind of thing once and you will be left with a question mark over your integrity. It's a short-term solution.

Never bounce a cheque. Once you've bounced a cheque, not only is your bank unimpressed, but you will never get favours from that supplier again. In my industry all the credit controllers regularly meet, so as soon as you bounce one cheque everybody knows about it. You will have a reputation either for being a crook or for not being in control of your business.

Property and location

When people ask how I can afford so many benefits for staff, I point out that Richer Sounds spends less than 1.5 per cent of its turnover on rent and rates. This compares with typically 10–20 per cent spent by the high-street multiples.

So we can afford good wages and holiday homes because we're not wasting money on property. We may have small shops in relatively downmarket locations, but they are staffed by a top quality workforce.

Keeping our overheads down by saving on property suits us very well. We invest in people, not buildings. It also conveys the right message to the customers. Our reputation is for selling good hi-fi at cheap prices and when customers see our shops in cheap locations, they are reassured that they are going to find a bargain.

We emphasise to customers our regret that our shops are small and explain that small shops equal low prices – and they love it.

This does not mean that we do not give a great deal of thought to the location of our shops, and we have often relocated several times within the same town to find the right spot. When we open a store, we can forecast how much money we are going to take based on that city's population size. So if a shop doesn't do well, it's either because of the location or because of the staff. We grow our own staff and know our managers, so the reason usually comes down to location.

In Leeds, for example, we knew within a few months that the shop wasn't doing as well as it should. We relocated it just 200 yards and the difference was a threefold increase in takings with only a small increase in rent.

Retailers' requirements will be different, so you have to know what is right for you. We don't want to be in shopping centres. Nearby parking space is more important for us than passers-by, because of the nature of our products. We look for visible sites – corner sites, if possible – and preferably freehold. We try to be in an inexpensive area, on an arterial route, and preferably in a student area too.

Lowering your overheads

I don't like spending any more than I need to on overheads and, in my experience, there is always scope for savings.

At Richer Sounds we have set up a very successful cost control group. This is a group of half a dozen people from around the company who are not involved with purchasing the product but who look at purchasing decisions with a critical eye. They question everything, from the cost of bin liners upwards. They are not involved with the nitty-gritty of purchasing – the reordering, seeing the reps – so they have no axe to grind.

In the same way, in a big organisation it would be worth creating a group that meets at four on a Friday afternoon with the task simply of looking at travel costs. They will ask a lot of awkward questions. When did the tender last go out? Why are we paying so much? Can we not get a better deal? The travel buyer will find them a pain in the neck, but also useful. To be effective, such groups must be sponsored at a high level in the organisation so that the purchasers take notice of them.

The best people for these groups are the archetypal *Exchange & Mart* (today's Craigslist, etc.) readers who always know about a deal. These are the people who have always heard about a shop down the road that's cheaper. They really enjoy this sort of thing, so use them.

Marketing

There is no point in selling £10 notes for a fiver if people don't know about it, so you need marketing.

Marketing is really every aspect of telling people about the business: advertising, the way you present the premises, the design of your stationery, and the way you look after your customers – because they tell other people. For me, customer service is the most effective form of marketing there is.

Advertising

The two things we want to convey in our Richer Sounds ads are our value for money and our friendliness. Many retailers forget about friendliness.

When you are considering press advertising, remember that what the ad agencies won't tell you is that lineage can be very cost effective.* They won't tell you that because they're on a percentage commission on the amount you spend.

* Lineage ads are small ads in the form of lines of type, as opposed to ones that are displayed or include pictures.

We always used to get a much better response from lineage than from display in publications like *Exchange & Mart*, the Sunday papers and *Private Eye*. People associate lineage with bargains.

The medium an ad is carried in is important for the product, too. We were famous – or notorious – for our ads in *Viz*. The fact was that these appealed enormously to young male customers, but as our customer base changed so did our advertising strategy. One Christmas we were advertising in *Viz*, *The Sunday Times* and *Gay Times*, and hoping the ads didn't get mixed up.

Measure your advertising response where you can. There is a lot you can do, such as include a coupon. We put in a Freephone number which enables us to measure the cost per response of every advertisement.

You don't always need an ad agency. We buy ad space direct, sometimes with our own credit card over the phone. You can get a better price if you pay straight away. The agencies sometimes get a good deal on space, but they might not pass the discount on to you anyway, preferring to keep the cream for their biggest clients.

Another problem with ad agencies is that they often won't work with more than one client per industry because of conflicts of interest, which means they have very little experience of your line of business.

There is also a lot of pressure on agencies to win awards. If your business, like mine, is not very glamorous and does not lend itself to arty ads, agencies might not put a lot of effort into your account. If they do and they win awards, you may still find that the adverts are great for the brand, but that they do not necessarily sell your products very well.

In-store catalogues

These are a hugely underestimated but incredibly effective form of advertising.

Anyone can make up a broadsheet to give out in a store telling your customers what you are selling, especially what offers you have at the moment. People always take them home and read them, and it amazes me that more businesses don't do this. We make sure no one leaves our shops without a catalogue. The more catalogue dispensers we put out, the more customers take one.

Our catalogue has grown into a thirty-two-page A4-size, full-colour magazine, all done by our in-house marketing department. It is a reference document for prices, opening times, phone numbers, addresses, brands and so on. It is also marvellous for giving customers more complex information. For instance, now that we sell home cinema equipment, we can educate customers about that in our catalogue too

We have invested heavily in our marketing department, equipping it with all the computers and software needed to produce this, as well as any other material. The catalogue now goes out every six weeks and has a circulation of up to 200,000 copies depending on the time of year, which is four times as much as the biggest hi-fi magazine in the country. This gives us great strength: we control the main channel of communication with our customers. We can convey to them exactly the message that we want.

The marketing tactic should obviously suit the product. When we first introduced our range of upmarket hi-fi, we started to advertise in upmarket magazines. We also used a different style for those pages devoted to the reference ranges in the catalogue. This went hand in hand with the styling of the demonstration rooms in our stores, which required the right ambience for selling more expensive products.

Growing the business

Lots of businesses start up, do well and then don't really know how to carry on. They don't know when the time is right to grow or how fast they should expand.

One of the tests should be financial controls. If you are producing reliable figures every month, that proves you have the self-discipline to go further.

Secondly, you must have your staff and managers in place. Thirdly, you should build on strong foundations. Never try to expand out of trouble. I've often heard companies say, 'If only we had another fifteen more stores to support head office, we would be OK.' That is nonsense. If you are having difficulties, the answer is to prune, not to expand.

I learnt this when my business grew too fast and it did not have the cash flow to maintain such growth. I cut stores back from sixteen to eleven and made sure I had a secure base before I expanded again.

Our pattern of growth has been small steps. We have added new stores and then had a period of consolidation, making sure they were all running well before we entered the next phase of expansion.

Entrepreneurs will want to try out new things and I've tried (and sometimes failed at) as many new ventures as anyone, but my advice would be: never risk more than you can afford. I've seen too many businesses risk everything on a new technology or a new brand, only for it to fail and bring them down.

Only by trying new things can you go forward, so you have to achieve a fine balance: stick to what you know, but continually try to improve it.

I believe in evolution, not revolution. Richer Sounds has evolved into entirely new areas, such as audio-visual, but we are still in a market we understand.

Growth should be slow and controlled, especially financially. It is like tending a bonsai tree: growing a really strong, solid object very slowly. I argue that what goes up slowly comes down slowly. If you build slowly, your company is far less likely to come crashing down.

Growing in steps has many advantages. If you are continually expanding it is very difficult to see and to measure the increase in costs and overheads. During the consolidation period, you can gain a true view of your position and bring your costs under control.

Whenever I see businesses undergoing drastic growth, I can see they have forgotten all the golden rules of *kaizen*. They are opening more sites, taking on more people, filling up with stock and opening the next one. They are not focusing on the detail that makes the profit.

They do not have experienced staff, they are not taking the time to train people properly, they haven't got the right stock in, they haven't got time to make the shop look right before they're on to the next one. They are not continually improving what they've got. The quicker you grow, the more details get forgotten.

Growth is not everything. Richer Sounds has been through two recessions and come out stronger each time. With low rent and rates, we can control our costs much better than firms with high fixed costs.

We found that in recessions, customers were willing to search us out to pay less. We became more aggressive about getting deals, which suited customers who were more value-conscious. So both times we took a bigger market share during recession. We try to look at it positively: overall, people might be spending 10 per cent less money, but what matters is that the proportion they spend on hi-fi, TVs and home cinema equipment is spent with us and not our competitors.

When the economy is not doing well, it is no good businesses sitting back moaning that times are hard and waiting for things to improve. They have to go out and drag the customers in.

10

Cultivate your culture

My ideas about motivation and management will
work for everyone, but none of the measures I've
suggested will go very far if your organisation does
not have the right culture.

It is no good picking up a couple of ideas and
trying to use them as quick fixes to jolly up your
workforce or improve your image. If you do not
have a culture of customer service, you cannot
create one overnight by telling your employees
to greet everyone with a smile. Both customers
and staff will know that it doesn't mean very
much. If you don't have a culture of caring for
your workforce, sending them birthday cards
won't fool them into thinking that you're a wonderful employer.

So what is culture and how do you build the
right one?

Culture is much more than image. It is not about
how you look, but what you do.

What makes Richer Sounds different from other electrical retailers? You might say it's our small, crowded shops and out-of-the-way locations, but really it is our priorities that are different. It's the fact that we focus on ongoing training, pay at the top of the market and provide some incredible benefits.

What we do in my company for employees is really a lot of little things, such as birthday cards, thank-you letters, and so on. Then there are also the big things, like the holiday homes and the Helping Hand hardship fund. In a way, they are all just gestures, but they add up to a culture.

None of the things we do for our staff is a quick fix. On their own, they won't produce a caring atmosphere. They are all signs, but together they send the message that when we say we will support people, we mean it and we back it with cash. The holiday homes and hardship fund show that we care about their well-being, not just about whether they can do a day's work for us.

When our staff are down the pub in the evenings with their friends, they know that other people don't work for companies that have holiday homes, sub-sidised healthcare and paid-for overseas trips for all of their long-service staff. They feel that they are working for a company that is different and special.

Having said that, hard work and honesty are just as much part of the culture as the caring element. It is part of the culture that everyone turns up punctually and works hard. It is part of the culture that theft is an unpardonable offence and that turning a blind eye to fraud is just as serious.

People make the culture and the culture is the people: the two things are interchangeable. Richer Sounds personnel are constantly feeding into and building on the culture through their suggestions, their attitude to the job and so on.

Initially, though, the culture is created by the people who run an organisation. My company's culture was very much born out of my own ideas and those of my colleagues about our responsibilities and about the place of a business in the wider society.

I do think that businesses are important in society, and that their contribution is not recognised enough, but I also think that businesses have social responsibilities, which some employers choose not to recognise.

Parents always seem to want their children to be doctors, not businesspeople, and especially not retailers. Personally, I can't stand the sight of blood and I think I've made a much better businessman than I ever would a doctor, but I do ask myself what I have contributed to the world.

The fact is that someone has to pay for doctors. An ethical business paying VAT, corporation tax and national insurance makes a sizeable contribution. Plus, there is all the income tax paid by me and my colleagues. I think people would feel proud if, at the end of every year, they were told how many doctors or teachers they and their company had paid for through their taxes.

I also think that one of the most important roles you can perform today is providing jobs. Unemployment is a terrible blight and decent, fairly paid jobs are a big contribution to a healthy society.

The reason people aren't falling over themselves with gratitude to employers is, of course, that not all jobs are decent or fairly paid, but I'm not in business to exploit my colleagues and I believe our attitude surveys prove that staff do not consider themselves exploited.

I hope that matters to customers, too. I don't think people favour organisations that treat their employees badly. For example, we never used to open our stores on a Sunday because when we asked the branches they were not keen on the idea. However, trading has moved on and they realise that times have changed since then, which has now resulted in us opening on Sundays. Rather than pushing our colleagues to work more days, we increased the number of colleagues per store and they work their days on a rotation basis with no one working more than a five-day week.

It's a pity there is not more public acknowledgement of good employers. You can win the Queen's

Award for exports, and successful businesspeople – if they are the right sort of pillars of society – end up with a CBE or a knighthood. However, suppose they were measured on their record as an employer rather than their company's performance on the stock market? Suppose they were praised for the taxes they paid rather than their cleverness in minimising their tax liability? Suppose we really knew what their employees thought of them? There might turn out to be some very different winners.

Businesses are also doing something worthwhile if they give better value than the competition. I like to think we are doing as much as we can for our customers by running an efficient business, keeping costs and therefore prices down, while at the same time trying to give great service.

Commerce and industry certainly have environmental responsibilities too. I would argue for balance here. Environmental awareness has to be within commercial reality. Businesses shouldn't be expected to lose money for environmental reasons, but they should be environmentally friendly wherever they have the opportunity.

These are the far-reaching, but often unseen, benefits of running a good business. In addition, Richer Sounds has its own charitable foundation and donates the highest percentage of profits to charity (currently 15 per cent) of any company we know of.

We maintain a low public profile for our charity work, but the important thing is that our staff know about it. The foundation is seen as part of the company and some people give a few days a month to work for it, which we pay them for.

The right culture is essential for good motivation. Many businesses have a mission statement, which is an important means of communicating to people what the organisation is doing, but a mission statement is not the culture.

Culture is the way people feel about the business and its activities. It's not about whether they are happy with the job, whether they agree with the company's aims, whether they respect its principles. It's about the way they think and operate.

I'm not trying to brainwash my staff and I'm not too bothered what they get up to in their own time, provided it doesn't affect what they do at work. I don't expect everyone to be a paragon of virtue, but I do expect integrity from them at work.

The Richer Sounds culture is built on integrity and loyalty. I have tried to create an organisation that has a common bond, a kind of overgrown family unit.

Other companies will have very different cultures, but every organisation should have a culture that is respected by its staff. It is important to employees that the bosses be seen to be responsible citizens. They are carrying the standard for their people at work and it does much to raise morale. If your business is involved in tax dodges, what message does that send employees about the standards of honesty they should apply at work?

I'm wary, though, of companies that try to use their culture to sell themselves. Once you set yourself up to be whiter than white – or, in these environmentally aware times, greener than green – you attract criticism and bad publicity at the first mistake you make.

The culture is something that exists for the benefit of you and your workforce, rather than something for the outside world to admire. Customers need only be concerned about how that culture translates into good service.

You cannot really separate culture from motivation. I believe that the reason our schemes have found favour with our staff is that they were offered in the right spirit. The holiday homes idea came to me when I was enjoying a break on the south coast. I thought, 'This is wonderful, how can I share it?' So the idea of holiday homes was born and soon afterwards the first one was opened near Eastbourne.

The Helping Hand fund and subsidised healthcare were brought in because I was concerned about the problems people were having getting medical help on the NHS. I thought it was important to systemise the way we help people within the organisation so they don't have to beg for assistance, but can claim it as a right.

I think the reason people find these benefits motivating is because they know the motives behind them are genuine. The culture has to come from the heart.

11

Ten ways to improve your business – today!

Now you've read the book, I hope it has inspired you to take a look at your own company and ask yourself how it can change for the better. I am positive that there are practical tips in this book that can help any organisation, but, more importantly, the book should have made you think about the way employees are treated and how managers can improve their management.

So where do you start? A few piecemeal measures won't really do much: you need to begin with the basics. Here's my plan of action, which anyone can use, from the smallest corner shop to the largest international company or the most complex government department.

1.   Talk to your staff and managers. Change in organisations is always greeted with suspicion, even cynicism, so start by telling everyone that you are seeking improvement and why.

Change can only happen when everyone is infected with enthusiasm for it.

2. Examine your mission statement. If you haven't got one, form a working party to draw one up.

3. Organise an attitude survey to find out what your employees really think and to discover the baseline from which to measure progress. Then repeat it at regular intervals.

4. Spend some serious time thinking about fun. How can you liven up the workplace? What goodies can you offer the people in your organisation? How can you treat yourselves better and create a happier atmosphere? Look at the reward structures – are they really designed to motivate your staff?

5. Go through the rule book and get rid of outdated regulations and meaningless traditions.

6. Set up a strategic customer service group to examine your customer service and how it can be improved, including gathering and monitoring performance data.

7. Devise ways of asking your customers what they think of your service at each stage of their contact with you.

8. Launch a suggestion scheme with the backing of the top person in the organisation. Get ideas flowing from everyone and use them!

9. Examine your recruitment guidelines and interview techniques. Find out what happens

on the first day for new recruits. Does motivation and communication start from day one? Design a welcome pack.

10. Ask yourself if you are happy with the value for money of your service or product. Could the quality be improved or the price lowered.

All efforts to introduce cultural change need the microscope and the knife: the microscope to examine every aspect of your organisation and its operations in detail, and the knife to make radical change where necessary.

These ten suggestions are just the start of a continuous process of discovering how you can manage and motivate people better, and also improve your service to customers. None of these changes can happen overnight, but all these ideas can be initiated today. And once they are initiated, follow them up – remember the principle of continuous improvement.

Good luck!

Appendices

The following pages show examples of some of the key tools we use at Richer Sounds: the questionnaire for our Annual Attitude Survey, the results of the 2016 survey and the questionnaire for customers we put on our receipts.

We are always looking to see how we can improve our questionnaires to get a better, more accurate response, and we have found from experience that these are the ones that work. There may be aspects of our questionnaires you can adapt for your own organisation, so feel free to use these ideas.

Appendix A

Employee Attitude Survey 2016

Dear Colleagues,

The attitude survey is conducted in order that you may express your views about working for the company and is therefore a cornerstone of our unique culture. It is very important that you answer this survey honestly as the success of the survey depends on your contribution. There are no wrong or right answers; this exercise is purely to help improve the company and your job satisfaction following on from the one completed last year and the changes we have implemented since then.

In return for your openness and participation I personally guarantee the complete confidentiality and anonymity of your response. If you wish you may leave this questionnaire anonymous, but please do state whether you are a sales or office-based colleague, etc.

Managers within the stores or departments will be responsible for ensuring colleagues have enough time to complete the questionnaires in work time. As I have said, in order for us to get a better understanding of the business and colleagues' feelings it is vital that everyone has their say. We are committed to responding to the issues raised by the survey and the results will be published for all colleagues to see. No facts relating to an individual will be discussed with anyone.

In the meantime, thank you for taking part in this survey and for contributing to our continuing success.

Yours,

Julian Richer

2016 Attitude Survey Results–Stores

305 colleagues completed the 2016 store survey (335 in 2015). Not every question was answered by every colleague.

(1)   How long have you been with the company?

	2016	2015
0–12 months	17%	19%
1–3 years	23%	25%
3–5 years	16%	13%
5–10 years	24%	23%
10 years +	20%	20%

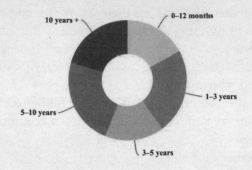

		Agree	Disagree	Don't Know	2015 Agree/ Disagree
(2)	My pay and benefits package I receive is fair for the job I do.	77%	9%	14%	55%/22%
(3)	I enjoy my job most of the time.	93%	3%	4%	87%/4%
(4)	If I was offered slightly more money (less than 10%) within the industry doing a similar job I would seriously consider taking it.	21%	44%	36%	33%/39%
(5)	It is fun working for Richer Sound most of the time.	91%	4%	5%	86%/5%
(6)	I am proud to say that I work for the company.	91%	2%	7%	83%/3%
(7)	I have good job security with the company.	80%	4%	16%	69%/8%
(8)	There is ample opportunity for promotion at Richer Sounds.	76%	10%	14%	65%/14%

		Agree	Disagree	Don't Know	2015 Agree/ Disagree
(9)	I will have to leave the company to advance my career in the next two years.	18%	39%	43%	*26%/30%*
(10)	If you have a potential personal issue, senior management are sympathetic and keen to help.	89%	1%	10%	*82%/4%*
(11)	The company is considerate of colleagues' family situations.	92%	1%	7%	*85%/3%*
(12)	Senior colleagues in the company are easy to talk to.	85%	5%	10%	*77%/8%*
(13)	The company acts as if colleagues are its most valuable resource.	74%	11%	15%	*66%/13%*
(14)	If the company makes a mistake I feel I have the opportunity to mention it.	75%	10%	15%	*66%/10%*
(15)	I am kept well informed of what is going on in the company regarding our company's progress.	93%	3%	4%	*94%/2%*
(16)	I feel I have opportunity to contribute to the company's development through team briefings, talking to senior colleagues, the suggestion scheme and the colleague council.	88%	2%	10%	*83%/5%*

		Agree	Disagree	Don't Know	2015 Agree/ Disagree
(17)	I feel encouraged to innovate in my job.	77%	8%	15%	70%/12%
(18)	I am generally aware of what other people do in the company.	90%	1%	9%	85%/5%
(19)	As a company we work very hard at delivering Customer Service.	93.7%	0.3%	6%	99%/1%
(20)	I feel procedures take preference over serving customers well.	15%	57%	28%	22%/54%
(21)	We work very much as a team in our store.	88%	7%	5%	85%/6%
(22)	I understand what is required of me in my job.	97%	1%	2%	98%/1%
(23)	I have received sufficient training to perform my duties to the required standard.	84%	8%	8%	79%/11%
(24)	We receive good customer service training at Richer Sounds.	94%	2%	4%	92%/3%
(25)	We receive good product and technical training.	89%	7%	4%	85%/7%
(26)	We receive good selling and procedures training.	92%	4%	7%	89%/4%
(27)	My store manager works hard to build us into a team.	72%	5%	23%	77%/9%

	Agree	Disagree	Don't Know	2015 Agree/ Disagree
(28) My store manager manages me effectively.	74%	3%	23%	77%/8%
(29) My store manager's style is a style I feel comfortable and relaxed with.	73%	6%	11%	78%/11%
(30) I have respect for my store manager.	83%	2%	15%	88%/4%
(31) My store manager's style of managing is a style that motivates me.	67%	7%	26%	71%/14%

	Manager	Deputy Manager	N/A
(32) Are you interested in promotion to…	24%	24%	52%

	Yes	No	On the waiting list	Would like to be included
(33) Have you completed the MDC course?	56%	29%	4%	11%
(34) If the right position within a store became available, where would you be willing to transfer to?				

North	10%
South	16%
Midlands	7%

Scotland	4%
Wales	3%
I would only be interested in the store I am currently based at	62%
Other (see comments)	22%

	No	Yes	Would you like to be referred for a second opinion through the company doctor?
(35) Is there a particular health complaint that you are worried about and would like a second opinion on?	92%	5%	3%

	Online in work	Online out of work	n/a
(36) Have you ever been impacted in any way by social media online, bullying, harassment or abuse? If yes, please describe the experience and how it made you feel.	0.3%	1.6%	98.1%

How did we do today?

In a continuous attempt to improve our service to you, I'd be extremely grateful if you'd spend a minute or so filling in this very short questionnaire. Our aim is to give you the very best service, because by doing so, we hope you'll recommend us to others and be a customer for life.

Please help us by giving your frank answers to a few simple questions because it is only by listening to what you say that we can improve our standards.

Good or bad comments, I'd like to hear them.

Julian Richer Julian Richer, Founder and Managing Director

First 50 responses picked monthly **WIN A £20 RS VOUCHER**	PLUS ONE LUCKY RESPONDENT WILL **WIN**	a 50 inch LED TV!

Key ★★★★★ Excellent ★★★★ Very Good ★★★ Good ★★ Poor ★ Very Poor

1. **Was your sales advisor friendly?**
   ○ ★★★★★   ○ ★★★★   ○ ★★★   ○ ★★   ○ ★

   If you needed technical help and the advisor was not familiar with your question, was he/she helpful in getting it for you?
   ○ ★★★★★   ○ ★★★★   ○ ★★★   ○ ★★   ○ ★

   Was your sales advisor too pushy? ○ Yes   ○ No

   How would you describe our overall service to you?
   ○ ★★★★★   ○ ★★★★   ○ ★★★   ○ ★★   ○ ★

   Would you recommend us to others?
   ○ Yes   ○ Maybe   ○ No

2. **Did you have trouble getting through to the store or to our dedicated Call Centre on the phone?**
   ○ Yes   ○ No   ○ Haven't tried

   If you had difficulties getting through on the phone, was the line
   ○ Engaged   ○ Unanswered   ○ Answerphone

3. **Branch Visited** _____ **Date Visited** _____

4. **How old are you?**
   ○ Under 18   ○ 18-25   ○ 26-40   ○ 41-50   ○ 51+

5. **Is this your first purchase from us?** ○ Yes   ○ No

   If yes, what brought you to us today?
   ○ Saw an ad   ○ Web   ○ Passing by   ○ Recommended

   If seen in an ad, which publication? _____

6. **Do you have any other comments, suggestions or complaints, however small? Your comments are especially appreciated on any area you rated poor or very poor**
   _____
   _____
   _____

You can add additional sheets or email customerservices@richersounds.com. We read every one sent to us. If you prefer, you can leave feedback online with a review. You will be emailed a link with your receipt.

Office Use:	RS/WP

Index